WHEN I AM
DEAD

Also by the Editor

WHEN I AM DEAD

The Writings of
George M. Teegarden

Raymond Luczak
Editor

Gallaudet University Press
Washington, D.C.

Gallaudet University Press
Washington, D.C. 20002
http://gupress.gallaudet.edu

Published 2007
Printed in the United States of America
Cover photograph: Courtesy of the Gallaudet University Archives
Cover design by Mona Z. Kraculdy

Library of Congress Cataloging-in-Publication Data

Teegarden, George M. (George Moredock), 1852–1936.
When I am dead : the writings of George M. Teegarden / Raymond Luczak, editor.
p. cm.
Includes bibliographical references.
ISBN 978-1-56368-348-0 (pbk. : alk. paper)
1. Deaf, Writings of the, American.   2. Deaf—Literary collections.
I. Luczak, Raymond, 1965–   II. Title.
PS3539.E165W45   2007
818'.409—dc22
2007006552

∞ The paper used in this publication meets the minimum requirements for
American National Standard for Information Sciences—Permanence of Paper
for Printed Library Materials, ANSI Z39.48-1984.

for John Lee Clark

Contents

Part One: Stories

In Pennsylvania

History Lessons

Life Lessons

Animal Stories

Retellings

People Stories

Personal Notes

Part Two: Poems

Acknowledgments

Nearly all of the stories were culled from George Teegarden's story collection *Stories, Old and New*, published by the Western Pennsylvania School for the Deaf in 1896. Nearly all of the poems chosen for this volume are from Teegarden's self-published *Vagrant Verses* in 1929. A few of his uncollected stories and poems were found in his school's newspaper, *The Western Pennsylvanian.* Some of the material was later reprinted in *The Tactile Mind.*

This project would not have been possible if not for John Lee Clark's extraordinary vision and André Pellerin's generous hospitality. Research suggestions from Brian C. Lewis and Katherine DeLorenzo proved fruitful. The thoughtful guidance and assistance provided by Ulf Hedberg and his staff at the Gallaudet University Archives was most appreciated. Michael La Rocca and Rita Rich have helped out in small but very significant ways. I truly appreciate Louis M. Miranda for allowing us to use his photograph of me. I am also grateful to Brenda Brueggemann, Jill Porco, Ivey Pittle Wallace, and John Van Cleve at Gallaudet University Press for making this book happen. As always, many thanks go to Tom Steele for his support in ways large and small, not only during this project, but also over the years.

The Slimmest of Evidence

An Open Letter to George M. Teegarden
March 11, 1852 — November 14, 1936

In the death of George M. Teegarden at Columbia Hospital last
Saturday night, Wilkinsburg [Pennsylvania] lost one of her most
eminent citizens.

A native of Jefferson, Greene County, Mr. Teegarden with his
parents moved to Iowa when he was a child. As a public school
pupil he lost his hearing at eleven years of age and was sent to
the Iowa State School for the Deaf. Later he attended Gallaudet
College, Washington, DC, the only college for deaf people in the
world. At the time of his graduation from Gallaudet the Western
Pennsylvania School for the Deaf was being organized at Turtle
Creek in 1876. Mr. Teegarden accepted an invitation to join the
teaching staff of the new school and remained with it until his
retirement forty-eight years later. He contributed more to the
development and increase in the value of the school than perhaps
any other one teacher in its history. He was instrumental in the
introduction of printing in the school. As teacher of printing at
one time he was the first editor of the *Western Pennsylvanian*. He
was the author of several textbooks and was a recognized leader
among the deaf nationally. Mr. Teegarden was a poet of unusual
ability, his poems portraying a keen appreciation of the beauties
of nature and a rare love of home and friends. Some of his sweetest poems were those he wrote in the last of the eighty-four years
of his life. Quiet and unassuming, Mr. Teegarden lived unosten-
tatiously, loved most by those who knew him best.

   —From the *Wilkinsburg Gazette*, November 1936[1]

Dear Mr. Teegarden,

Although you are long dead and have become a secondhand
memory for the children of the students who once knew
you, I feel compelled to reach across the decades from your simpler
time to my far more complex era.

I

Obviously I was never among your many students at the Western Pennsylvania Institution for the Deaf and Dumb (as the current Western Pennsylvania School for the Deaf was then known), but I would have loved being your student. You taught at the school for *forty-eight* years! That says a lot about your devotion and commitment to teaching, but that's not why I wish I had been one of your students.

No, I'd like to go further than that—much further than that.

Like many deaf children, I had parents who never signed, and I was forbidden to sign. That ban lasted until I turned fifteen and dared to learn signs on my own. I have often wondered whether the quality of my growing up would have been better if I'd had parents who tried to understand me and my needs *as I was*, not as they wanted me to be. You see, Mr. Teegarden, I was raised by a variety of foster fathers during the week for more than nine years. I had to commute two hours on weekends to attend a speech-oriented program for deaf children during those years. These foster fathers never understood me or encouraged me to be myself. Sure, my biological father wanted me to learn more than anything, and that I did. I never got to know him too well because he was too busy working as a meat cutter to feed his family of eleven along with a Siberian husky. What I didn't realize growing up was how much I needed another deaf writer in my life, someone who didn't think it was enough just to write, but who made a point of choosing words carefully. You would have made a terrific father and a writer-mentor to a grateful son and budding writer.

I have been so spoiled by this age, a time when communication is instantaneous and seems glib enough to explain the human condition through 30-second sound bites and advertiser-fed iconography. However, the human condition is far too complex to be explained so briefly; it can only be experienced. When I read your stories, I feel very much like a child, not because the language you use predates the simple elegance set forth in William Strunk's and E. B. White's *Elements of Style*, but because there is something about your style that *allows* me to be a child. I don't have to be obsessed with the magic

2

and potions concocted by J. K. Rowling in the Harry Potter books or with exploring the parallels between C. S. Lewis's Narnia tales and the New Testament. I can be someone once young who can see both the beauty of imagination and the ugliness of life without dwelling on their moral implications. Love and death are given the same weight in your stories. You were not afraid to make your presence felt through a sharp admonishment at the end of your cautionary tales.

You so clearly saw your role, not only as a teacher but also as a father at an institution where so many deaf students were separated from their hearing parents. It is not surprising that you had only one child, Alice, who herself went on to become a teacher of the deaf in White Plains, New York. Nowhere in my research could I ascertain whether you'd named your daughter after Lewis Carroll's most famous literary creation, or even after Alice Cogswell, Laurent Clerc's most famous pupil, but if so, neither reason would surprise me. Your love for Alice was clear for all to see in the poems you dedicated to her. Yet I could not find a poem specifically about your wife. How did you truly feel about her? Was she an obligation, and your daughter a joy? I find it odd that you do not mention your wife in your writing.

Each of my favorite of your stories feels like a new card pulled out of an ever-shuffling deck. The framing around the image looks the same, but when I read closer, I see more in the imagery you painted in your stories. You have a focus; you write so cleanly and directly that the stories are actually fully conceived "short-shorts," a fiction genre that has been an obsession of mine for a long time. I don't think that short-shorts were considered a genre in your time because very few people in those days thought that the work of living writers was worthy of academic and cultural dissection. The short-short is difficult because of its rigid limitations. Most people agree that such a story should be one thousand words or less and should fulfill the minimal story requirements of having a beginning, a middle, and an end. Yet it is a marvelous form because all the best writers—no matter how long their work may seem—have perfected the art of *condensation* in thought and meaning. If one can master the short-short, one definitely can write better, longer works of fiction. The same is true of poetry because poets who master the various form limitations involving meter, rhyme, and structure can generate a conciseness that may be difficult to achieve yet pays off handsomely for the reader.

There's something else at work in your stories. In her book *American Childhood,* Anne Scott MacLeod points out that in the era before 1860

> children's stories were static and repetitious. There were few departures from conventional opinion, few surprising points of view. Controversy was as rare as genius in the literature.
>
> The focus of the stories was extremely narrow. They were written to teach, and specifically, to teach morality. . . . Characterization and plots were purposefully flat. Nineteenth-century theorists of child nurture were tireless in pointing out that children learned much better by example than by precept . . . . Since complexity could only have obscured the messages, characterization was simple and it was always easy to identify the good and bad models. Lazy, fretful Louisa was contrasted with her cheerful, industrious cousin, and the story showed how the differences in their temperaments shaped their lives. . . . In story after story, good character was contrasted with bad, and appropriate conclusions drawn.[2]

If MacLeod's comments about the state of children's literature prior to 1860 are true, and if you had as voracious an appetite for reading as I imagine you did, then I am sure you saw through these predictable narratives. Instead, it seems that you sought to jolt the reader by describing mishaps in different ways. MacLeod observes that

> what small excitement there was in the stories was furnished by the consequences of childish misbehavior. A girl whose fondness for sweets took her into the pantry by night to lick the honey jar managed to burn down the house with the candle she left there. A boy who skated on thin ice against all parental warning fell through and narrowly escaped death by drowning. There was, in fact, a plethora of narrow escapes in the literature, all fitting and frightening results of moral error. But near-disaster was usually close enough.[3]

Mr. Teegarden, this is true of many of your stories. You do not shirk from the reality of death. You deal with it in a matter-of-fact way in your stories. This is hardly surprising because in your time many people worked on farms and accepted the death of animals as part of life. It was also true that parents often created large families as a way of sustaining a viable workforce on the land should some of the children die young due to various illnesses. I still wonder, however, how you taught your students about the realities of your times. You barely mention them anywhere in your work. For example, you don't discuss the rise of industrialization, the migration of agricultural workers to urban factories, and the institutionalization of Jim Crow laws and segregation in the South after the Civil War. To my knowledge, you never mention the fact that during the years you taught at the Western Pennsylvania School for the Deaf, Pittsburgh was very much a bustling city due to the thriving steel industry. Some of your poems on the idylls of nature may have been an indirect response to the rise of the factory smoke in the Pittsburgh air, which earned the city the nickname "the Smoky City."[4] More important, I was unable to find any reference in your work to the infamous Second International Congress on Education of the Deaf in September 1880, also known as the Milan conference. The American delegation and one British delegate cast the only two votes in opposition to the ban of sign language. The two most influential resolutions passed at Milan were

1. The Convention, considering the incontestable superiority of speech over signs (1) for restoring deaf-mutes to social life, and (2) for giving them a greater facility of language, declares that the method of articulation should have the preference over that of signs in the instruction and education of the deaf and dumb.
2. Considering that the simultaneous use of signs and speech has the disadvantage of injuring speech and lip-reading and precision of ideas, the Convention declares that the pure oral method ought to be preferred.

These resolutions passed despite the fact that American residential schools for the deaf had been successful in using sign language to educate their students. As a result of the Milan conference, the quality of education for deaf students in the United States began its eventual downward spiral when deaf students were forced to learn via the oral method during their peak years of language acquisition. Alexander Graham Bell, the inventor of the telephone, which had accidentally come about as he attempted to create a hearing aid, was a key influence on the conference. He persuaded many educators of the deaf to ban the use of sign language in their teaching of deaf students. He thought they should redirect their energies in using the oralist method as the main way to educate deaf students. Mr. Teegarden, how did you really feel about Mr. Bell and the oralists? Were you too afraid to speak out against the well-funded and well-oiled oralist propaganda machine of the Alexander Graham Bell Association and its *Volta Review*, the oralist *Pravda* of its day? Or were you simply afraid of losing your job? If so, I'm sorry to report that these possible reasons for not speaking out have not changed much from your time to mine.

When I first came to Gallaudet College (now University) as a freshman in 1984, I learned quickly about the signing deaf community's long-standing hatred of Alexander Graham Bell and his campaign against sign language. Why, those eight resolutions passed in Milan back in 1880 had nearly killed off the use of sign language in formal deaf education! How could Bell support such a crusade against sign language when he himself was the son of a deaf mother and the husband of a deaf woman? Bell also opposed intermarriage between deaf people and supported eugenics as a way of eliminating hereditary deafness, which he viewed a most undesirable trait. Your people must have felt intensely betrayed by such an insider who had been around deafness all his life.

Not all is completely silent with you, Mr. Teegarden. You celebrate in poetry and prose the achievements of hearing men, such as Thomas Hopkins Gallaudet and the Reverend John G. Brown, who worked hard to make their institutions succeed. Yet it is rather telling that you do not celebrate the accomplishments of deaf leaders in print as much as you do the others. Such lapses in your writing only makes me wonder whether you felt that hearing people were somehow superior to deaf people.

Mr. Teegarden, I wish I could have come to you with my early rambling attempts at fiction and poetry. You could have shown me the best way to write more economically. Less is more, and careful word choices are crucial. (Another note to myself: Stop after the first "more.") You would have understood that each sentence written is a simple brick that contributes to the solidity of each paragraph until the story becomes an unshakable brick house. (Perhaps you find my metaphors awkward, Mr. Teegarden, but metaphors are my way of explaining the untranslatable in precise terms.) Perhaps you would have told me to keep my opinions out of my writing and allow my facts to speak for themselves. Please forgive me. It is not every day that I write a letter to a writer whose work intrigues me. But the more that time passes with documents, letters, and people who once knew you disappearing, the more obscure your image becomes.

Just who *are* you, Mr. Teegarden?

Reading all about you in the issue of the *Western Pennsylvanian* published in your memory made me so envious of that golden age of deaf education in which literacy and intellectual development were valued above all else. It is clear that you believed in those things more than anything else, and you also loved teaching. You worked with two other people to write *Raindrop*, a collection of stories for use with deaf students. Yet there is no indication in the work of who wrote which stories. Even though I did not include any material from *Raindrop* in this work, the book's initial success eventually led to your publishing your own book, *Stories, Old and New*. I have mined that book for material here, along with poems from your self-published work *Vagrant Verses*.

Ironically, it is not words themselves that interest you. You are not a stylist by nature. When you are, it is by sleight-of-hand—pun unintended and intended at the same time—that I would be hard pressed to categorize it. Your style is not as easily definable as, say, Ernest Hemingway's. Still, I don't see you as the kind of a writer who struts around the room like a peacock but more as one who does not particularly want to be noticed. You would, however, want your *thoughts* and *ideas* lingering in the intimate air between the reader and the page. Your style may be quite inconspicuous, but your stories are extraordinary in ways that may not seem obvious to the average reader.

The uniqueness of your stories, Mr. Teegarden, lies in the fact that you never wrote for the hearing reader. Your story "The Ugly Aunt" is a good example of your storytelling abilities. It reflects the fact that you wrote as a person who had to communicate in both English and American Sign Language (ASL) every day. Let's look at the first few sentences of the story:

> Long ago there was a little girl whose parents were dead and who had no brothers and sisters. This poor orphan was left all alone without friends to take care of her. She had no relations. Her name was Geraldine. She was very beautiful and she was always anxious to learn and willing to work. This was well for she had to earn her own living.[5]

The ASL-familiar reader will find these sentences incredibly easy to transliterate. A *possible* translation in ASL glosses follows:

> Before short girl parents dead none brothers sisters. Girl abandon alone none friends take-care none family. Her name G-E-R-A-L-D-I-N-E [name sign Geraldine]. Herself wow beautiful herself eager learn willing work. Good because earn money survive.

While the English grammar of your stories seems slightly convoluted and repetitious in places, the proper ASL grammar remains *intact* in transliteration so there is no need to *translate*. For the uninitiated reader who knows little about ASL, it must be emphasized that ASL is not "English on the hands"; it is not only a language on the hands but a legitimate language on par with spoken languages. ASL has its own set of idioms, grammatical rules, and expressions that can be translated into English.

You wrote these stories to teach your students the importance of improving their reading and writing skills. What strikes me most about your stories is your ability to combine both ASL and English so flawlessly. Your stories are *almost* transliterations to the point where I, as an ASL user, can imagine you standing in front of a chalky blackboard and signing the stories smoothly and effortlessly. You were able to convey phrases in ASL in ways that your students could understand. In those days no one argued over whether your signing was ASL or Pidgin English; it was just *a* sign language for the deaf. I'd be very intrigued to know your thoughts about Dr. William Stokoe's groundbreaking assertion in 1960 that ASL is a bona fide language unto itself and not an inferior backup for those who have failed to master the art of lipreading English. I wonder how you would have felt about ASL had it been legitimized during your lifetime. I am sure you would always have continued to sign, but I know that English was equally as important to you as an educator.

Even though I may write in English for the stage and the screen, it is still difficult for me to write in a way that requires very little translation from English to ASL. My personal solution to this problem is to use ASL glosses in writing to represent signed conversation. It is not an elegant solution, however.

That is why, Mr. Teegarden, I am in awe of you as a young child might be in awe of his father, a man who clarifies the differences between right and wrong and who isn't afraid to act on those differences. You were unflaggingly realistic and yet so supportive of us deaf children. Many of us never received this unconditional acceptance from our non-signing parents. I suspect you, as an alumnus of a deaf residential school, understood and appreciated your strong bond with the deaf children living at the Western Pennsylvania School for the Deaf. Otherwise, you would have gone elsewhere after graduating from Gallaudet. But you stayed at the school for five decades. You held the same job all that time and took on additional teaching and editing duties at the print shop. Who knows how many students you influenced by remaining in one place. I was deeply moved by the tremendous affection with which students and other alumni wrote about you in the pages of the *Western Pennsylvanian* upon your retirement from the school. You really were the father that they never had because their home was where their hands felt most comfortable. You knew their language, and you weren't afraid to use the power of ASL to convey simple and complex English concepts.

You wrote a short book called *Common Words in Different Senses*. Many examples of the same verb used in different contexts appeared in this book. For instance, you listed many possible uses of the same English verb *gathered*.

The men gathered apples.
The boys gathered up sticks.
The dog gathered the sheep.
The people gathered at the church.
A mob gathered on the street.
The reporter gathered news.
The seamstress gathered the skirt at the top.
The boy gathered his wits together.[6]

I am sure you would have translated the verb's meaning in each sentence into ASL. I would not be surprised if you knew that this was an effective way to teach English to ASL users. I can easily imagine you, Mr. Teegarden, standing in front of your class, fingerspelling the verb *gathered*, and then translating each sentence into ASL, again while fingerspelling the verb *gathered*. Your students would have learned the word's varied meanings in two languages this way. You would have used ASL signs to convey the different meanings for a particular English word, demonstrating that meaning depends on context. Conversely, you would have told your students that one sign could be translated into several English words. For example, the sign for "street," could be written as *street, road,* or *avenue*. In short, so much depends on context. Your goal was to teach your students to communicate effectively in both languages. That hasn't changed one iota from your time to mine.

The students who put together the school newspaper, the *Western Pennsylvanian*, wanted to enter the printing and lithography industry, two of the most viable occupations for deaf people in those days.

The periodical was one of many produced by the deaf community all over the country. So many newspapers were published during the period from the 1850s to the 1940s, that it is regarded as the "Golden Age of the Little Paper Family."[7] The fact that articles in the *Western Pennsylvanian* often quoted, with acknowledgments, from other publications of the Little Paper Family shows a genuine sense of community in the deaf world. I believe this spirit came directly from mentors like yourself who taught these deaf students how to print. You realized how crucial it was for any deaf printer or writer to master English. You knew this mastery would empower them to write their own stories of prejudice and discrimination for others in the deaf community to read. In the "Golden Age of the Little Paper Family," literacy was not only paramount, it was self-evident among deaf people. It is peculiar, then, to note that so few deaf people had books published during this same period. I wonder, Mr. Teegarden, how were you treated as a deaf *writer*? And why did you use the amusing pseudonym T. G. Arden for some of your published works? How I wish you could answer such questions!

When I began putting your stories into my computer, I realized that things have come full circle for me. I may not be a lithographer, but like the deaf lithographers of yesteryear, I have prepared this book myself for a publishing company in the field of deafness. Through my mastery of English and an understanding of the mechanical and technical aspects of publishing, I have the power to change the world in a very small, almost inconspicuous, way. Mr. Teegarden, I have no doubt that you would have shown me how I could write this or that sentence in a better way. You would have insisted that I participate in the Gallaudet Literary Society, were it still in existence. The members held debates before three judges who decided which side had the stronger argument. Storytelling and poetry readings followed the debates. It would have been an extraordinary opportunity to grow intellectually and artistically in both English and ASL.

Oh, Mr. Teegarden, at times I don't know when to stop writing. I find the computer a necessary evil. On one hand, I think it is the best thing that ever happened to writers. Complaints about how tiring it is to write in longhand or to punch manual typewriter keys have disappeared. Suddenly, there is no pain involved with writing nonstop. One no longer has to worry about getting to the bottom of the page or having to go back to the middle of a paragraph to put down that perfect sentence. On the other hand, the computer has made it too easy to ramble on about nothing in particular. We writers today do not know when to shut up. But you *did* know when and how to stop. I have come to believe that good writing these days is more about knowing *when* to stop than what to say. That is why I find your stories such a breath of fresh air—they are short, painless, and told with a sense of wonder. Also, the time-consuming reality of setting type in your day meant that your writing had to be precise before you turned it in. Your words were set in metal; a publisher couldn't automatically repaginate if you cut a whole paragraph in the middle of a chapter.

It reminds me again that good writing is all about *careful choice*. The perfect adjective can do the work of three peppery adjectives, which, when placed together, leave a flat aftertaste. But you have gone further than mere word choice. You are deeply interested in *moral* choices, the very stuff of literature. Too few writers today explore moral choices in their work; it is almost as if the very concept is embarrassing. Mr. Teegarden, you are resolute in your moral views of the world and you condemn bad decisions without condemning the people involved.

The fact that you were deaf means a great deal to me because, like many deaf people, I am not from a deaf family in which members pass deaf cultural traditions down the generations. I agree with your friend George Veditz, the first leader of the National Association of the Deaf (NAD), who understood the importance of preserving our cultural heritage in every way, including film. That is why I felt I had no choice but to learn how to shoot and edit movies. I did not do this because I think being a filmmaker is a cool profession in today's media-oriented culture. (I can assure you that the long hours and the level of dogged persistence required is anything but cool.) I do this because I want to preserve *something* for the deaf child of the future who, even if fitted with cochlear implants, will learn that she lacks something in her life until she experiences the full power of being deaf and the joy of communicating through signing. Even though you lost your hearing at age 11, I would like to think that you feel the same way, that being deaf is totally fine.

This is where I stop short. You almost never mention deafness in your writing, let alone your own life-changing experience of losing your hearing. Granted, with your awareness of Deaf culture, it would seem a no-brainer to me for a writer like yourself to launch into lengthy discussions about your experiences growing up at the Iowa School for the Deaf, coming of age at Gallaudet, and working at the Western Pennsylvania School of the Deaf. I have not been able to find much mention of these experiences in your writing that I have seen to date. I think you did not discuss your deafness because you lived and worked primarily with deaf users of ASL and, therefore, your deafness wasn't as much of an issue as it might otherwise have been. At first, I wondered whether you felt the same isolation as I sometimes have as a deaf writer, but I don't think so. You had charge of a printery, and you also wrote for the school newspaper. You participated in what might be called "Deaf culture" today. You probably would be totally surprised by how deaf people regard themselves today—with justifiable pride. You also would have been pleased with the degree of research into our history, language, and culture present in academia today.

I am curious to know why you shifted your focus from writing stories to writing poetry after the publication of *Stories, Old and New*. I do not understand this because, frankly, some of the poetry is not particularly good or revelatory, even though you show good technique and command of meter. This reminds me of Thomas Hardy, who, when his great novels *Tess of the d'Urbervilles* and *Jude the Obscure* horrified both readers and critics, decided that he would achieve better acceptance as a poet. He wrote a great deal of poetry, which he held in high regard. Unfortunately, most of it is not very good. I wonder if you were like Mr. Hardy in this respect. After all, you self-published your collection *Vagrant Verses*. It is unclear why you stopped writing short stories; the few you did write later appeared sporadically in the *Western Pennsylvanian*.

I have another quandary when trying to ascertain your true nature. You were born in 1852 and, therefore, came of age during the Victorian era when one did not talk directly about those things in life deemed unseemly. Or if one did, it was always couched in coded language that I must work to understand. Judging from your appearance—a stern-looking man with a mustache and a tight pair of wire-rimmed glasses—I think you probably would have felt extremely uncomfortable talking directly about sex and emotions. I note, however, that some of your stories are downright violent and nasty. Despite your seemingly stoic nature, you wrote the following letter as a token of your thanks to the Western Pennsylvania School for the Deaf upon your retirement.

To my Friends:

You "retired" me from the position I have held at this School for some years and you did it with gifts and kind words of commendation as one does to an old friend when he sets out on a long journey into unknown lands—expressions of appreciation and sincere friendship. For this I thank you.

True friends are those who encouragingly bear with one's faults and shortcomings in thought and understanding and these I feel I have had in abundance. They have been an asset in the business of life and made it worthwhile so I can but feel that I have been abundantly blessed. Through the years of service here, I cannot remember one who has not "shown himself, or herself, friendly."

A very wise man has said, "The making of friends, who are real friends, is the best token we have of a man's success in life." Judging by this standard, and by your expressions of esteem, I can feel, I have attained to a fair measure of success in life and I do appreciate the encouragement meted out by my friends.

Again I thank you one and all.

G. M. Teegarden[8]

This letter reflects your kind nature that comes through in your other writing. Fathers are often perceived as relics of an earlier time and, therefore, allegedly have little to offer their children except to inspire scorn, fear, and possibly, pain in their souls. Because men are supposed to be strong, burying their emotions deep inside creates an invincible facade. I wish I could know what you really felt growing up, especially after you lost your hearing and learned ASL at the Iowa School for the Deaf, but that is the psychobabble part of me seeking explanations for the mystery of you. I will never truly know the father figure you so clearly were except through the stories and poems in this book. I do know that your writings reflect your nature and inspired a great deal of affection and respect from generations of your students.

I sensed your omnipresence when I read your stories, yet I continue to have questions about you. Who were you to have penned these words? Why did you choose to tell these particular stories? And those poems, which seem designed to please more than anything? Even though you wrote many stories derived from the Bible, how did you come to hold such different worldviews? You are mysterious, Mr. Teegarden, and I am afraid that after being raised on today's diet of instant tell-all, I find myself hungry to know you better. The stories and poems you published provide the slimmest of evidence of the man you were. I hope that future deaf writers will read your works and feel inspired to create a language of their own, knowing that you did it so well before.

Your writing was of such an understated achievement that I was compelled to put together a collection of your stories and poems. I imagine that you would feel embarrassed by my efforts if you were alive today. But fathers, when they do their job well, often remain unsung heroes.

Not so, George Moredock Teegarden. I sing to you now.

Sincerely,
Raymond Luczak

Notes

1. George M. Teegarden obituary. Reprinted in the *Western Pennsylvanian* (28 January 1937), 75.

2. Anne Scott MacLeod, *American Childhood: Essays on Children's Literature of the Nineteenth and Twentieth Centuries.* (Athens, GA: University of Georgia Press, 1994), 89–91.

3. MacLeod, *American Childhood,* 91–92.

4. http://www.smokycity.com/about.html#Pittsburgh

5. George Moredock Teegarden, "The Ugly Aunt," in *Stories: Old and New.* (Edgewood Park, PA: The Institution for the Deaf, 1896), 10.

6. George Moredock Teegarden. *Common Words in Different Senses* (Edgewood Park: The Institution for the Deaf, n.d.), 26.

7. John Vickrey Van Cleve and Barry A. Crouch, *A Place of Their Own: Creating the Deaf Community in America.* (Washington, DC: Gallaudet University Press, 1989), 98.

8. George Moredock Teegarden, letter, *Western Pennsylvanian,* May 15, 1924.

Part One

STORIES

In Pennsylvania

Horned Toads

One day a young lady who lived near Pittsburgh received a small box by mail. When she opened it she found it full of dry dirt and small stones. She did not know what it meant. She examined the box carefully. Then she began to stir up the dirt in the box with her fingers. Soon she discovered several curious-looking creatures among the dirt and stones. At first she was startled, then she looked at them more carefully. They were horned toads. The lady thought them very funny. She caught flies and fed them. As soon as they were fed, the toads would bury themselves in the dirt again. The lady kept the toads several months and showed them to all her friends. They were quite a curiosity. They were sent from California. Horned toads have little hard lumps on their heads and bodies. They seem to be very lazy and do not hop about like common toads. They act a little like lizards.

Gusky

There is a young elephant in Schenley Park, in Pittsburgh. She is called Gusky, being named after Mrs. J. M. Gusky who presented her to the park authorities. She is an intelligent animal and has a very good memory as this story will show.

Many children visit the Zoological Garden in the park and, of course, they always go to see Gusky. The elephant likes to have the children visit her for they always bring something good to eat; such as peanuts, cake, and fruit. She takes the eatables from their hands and never hurts them.

One day several children were feeding Gusky. One small boy got a stick with a nail in the end of it. He stuck buns on the nail and handed them to the elephant. The boy was tricky. When Gusky was about to take a bun he suddenly twisted the stick and gave it a jerk and ran the nail into the animal's trunk. After that he ran away and did not come back for several months. When he came back again he went to the elephant stable to see Gusky. Perhaps he thought he would play another trick on her, but he did not.

As soon as he came into the stable the elephant recognized him. She ran up and caught him with her trunk. She crowded him against the wall of the stable and tried to trample on him. She trumpeted loudly and the boy screamed as hard as he could. The elephant's keeper heard them and rushed into the stable. He commanded Gusky to let the boy go but she refused to obey. The keeper seized a pitchfork and jabbed the elephant's neck and shoulder with it. Then she dropped the boy and he was dragged out of her reach. Gusky remembered what the boy had done to her six months before and wanted to punish him. I do not think the boy will want to visit Gusky again. It is not safe to fool with elephants because they will remember it and have revenge whenever they get a chance.

A Kind Dog

A man and his wife, living in Pennsylvania, had a quarrel. While they were quarreling, their baby, four months old, was thrown out of the kitchen window. The parents did not care for the child, and kept on quarreling.

A large Newfoundland dog, which lived nearby, passed the house and found the baby lying on the ground. He picked it up with his teeth and carried it carefully across a creek to his kennel. He laid it down in the straw and watched it.

By and by, the man and his wife stopped quarreling. Then they began to think about their baby. They could not find it, and became alarmed. They searched for two hours for their little one. At last the father heard a low cry from the dog's kennel and went there. He found his baby in the kennel, kicking about in the straw and the good-natured dog watching it.

The man carried the baby home and I think he felt ashamed because the dog was kinder to the baby than its parents were.

Playing with Powder

Tom and his three brothers lived on a small farm in Pennsylvania. They had a friend, named George, who lived in the village near their home. The boys were together a great deal, and like all boys, got into a good deal of mischief. One day they saw some Irishmen blasting rocks and liked to hear the report of the blast, to see the flash from the powder and the pieces of rock fly in the air. Soon after this the boys decided to have some fun and play with gunpowder and make a blast like the quarrymen. Tom's father kept an old-fashioned rifle and powder-horn. The horn was full of powder. George persuaded Tom to get his father's powder-horn. Tom got the horn without his parents knowing it. Then the boys all went to a lane near the house and dug a hole in the bank. They also built a fire of some sticks nearby.

George took the powder-horn and poured a handful of powder into the hole in the bank. He then took a live coal out of the fire and dropped it into the hole, while Tom and his brothers ran off to a safe distance.

Now it happened there was no fire on one side of the coal, so the powder did not ignite. The fire was on the upper side of the coal, as it fell into the hole, so it did not touch the powder. The boys waited awhile and as the powder did not burn, they all came up closer to the little mine in the bank. Then George took the powder-horn and went up close to the hole. He held the horn over it and poured the powder in a stream into the hole. It fell upon the coal of fire and all at once there was a loud report and the dirt and gravel flew in every direction. The blast had gone off and so had a large part of George's pants. The flash from the powder went up his trouser-legs and tore them off. His legs were terribly burned and blistered all over. The powder-horn was burst in two in his hand and the pieces flew away. One piece struck Tom on the forehead and the other piece struck one of his brothers. They were not hurt much but they were very much frightened. George ran home and the doctor dressed his burns. It was several weeks before he got well. The boys did not want to experiment with gunpowder again very soon. They had had all the experience they wanted. This is a true story and happened a good many years ago.

A Bad Cat

A little girl lived in Munhall, near Homestead. She was only three years old. One day she was playing with a big black tomcat in the kitchen. The two got along very pleasantly together for a while. Pretty soon the child got a pair of scissors and looked about for something to cut. She noticed the cat's long whiskers. She probably thought they were too long, so she decided she would trim them. She cut them too close and the cat became very angry, and made a fierce attack on the child. The child's mother ran to save it from the cross cat. Then the cat left the child and sprang upon the woman. It tore her body terribly with its sharp claws and tried to catch her by the throat with its teeth. The woman threw up her hand to protect her face and got one of her fingers in the cat's mouth. She could not make the cat let go. Just then the woman's husband came home from work. He seized the cat by the throat and choked it to death. The cat held on to the finger until it was almost dead. The woman's finger was badly torn and the doctor had to amputate it. Perhaps the cat was offended because it was robbed of its fine whiskers.

A Little Spartan

Not long ago a little girl was hurt by a street car in Pittsburgh. It happened she ran against the side of the car and was drawn under the rear wheels before the car could be stopped. She was pinioned under the heavy truck and was badly hurt, but she did not scream or cry out. She bore the pain very heroically while they were getting her from under the wheels. When they got her out, it was found that she was badly cut and bruised about the head and face, and one leg was almost cut off. She bore the pain as bravely as a Spartan and never made a complaint. While waiting for the ambulance she lay in the conductor's arms. She noticed the motor man's watch chain and asked for it. It was given to her. She held it in her hand and smiled. "Don't saw off my leg, doctor," she said, as soon as one came to help her. She was taken to the hospital where the doctors did all they could for her, but in the evening she died from her injuries. It was pathetic to witness how patiently she bore her suffering. Her name was Alma Beck, and she was ten years old.

A Strange Accident

Mr. White, a farmer, was walking through the woods near New Castle, Pennsylvania, when he heard groans as of someone in trouble. At first he was startled and listened attentively. Then he went in the direction of the sounds and came to a large chestnut tree. He looked up into the tree and saw a man hanging by the seat of his trousers on a broken branch, thirty feet from the ground.

Mr. White was very much surprised to see the man hanging up there. He shouted to the man but he did not answer. He was unconscious. Then Mr. W. called some men and they took the man down. They carried him to a farmhouse and laid him to a bed.

By and by, the man regained consciousness and told them how he happened to be hanging on the tree. He told them his name was Harry Hoyt and that his home was near Pittsburgh. He was out of work and was going about the country looking for something to do. As he walked along the road he noticed the chestnut tree and climbed it to get some nuts. While he was picking the nuts the limb, on which he stood, broke. He fell a short distance when his trousers caught on the broken limb. He was thus suspended in the air, and could not free himself. He hung there in the tree all the afternoon. He called and called for help but nobody heard him. By and by, it became dark and at last he became unconscious. He was very glad to be safe again. If Mr. White had not heard him he might have died in the tree. It was a strange accident.

Dangerous Coasting

Some boys were coasting down a steep hill on the road which crossed the railroad track. The road was very icy and smooth so that the sleds ran very fast. The boys enjoyed the sport very much. It happened as one boy was going down the hill, a train of cars came along on the railroad. The boy was lying on his stomach on his sled and going at a rapid rate. He saw the cars but he could not stop his sled. On he went and he felt sure he would run into the train and be ground to pieces under the wheels. When he was close to the cars he shut his eyes and waited for the shock. The train was running very fast but nothing happened. His sled ran on down the hill. He opened his eyes and found that he was safe while the train was almost out of sight. He wondered how it happened. He found out that, just as he expected to strike the cars, he had shot under them between the wheels. He was going so fast that the wheels did not catch him, so he was safe. It was a miraculous escape.

History Lessons

Thomas Hopkins Gallaudet

Thomas Hopkins Gallaudet was born in Philadelphia on the 10th of December 1787. His ancestors were Huguenots from France. When he was thirteen years old his parents moved to Hartford, Connecticut. Mr. Gallaudet was never very strong in body. When he was a boy, he loved to study. He was very bright and industrious. He learned very fast. He entered Yale College in 1805. He was a deep thinker and talked like a person much older than he was. In his youth he wrote verses for his own pleasure. Some of his poems have been printed.

After he left College, Mr. Gallaudet studied law one year. His health was not good so he had to stop studying law. Soon after this, he became a tutor in Yale College where he remained two years. He next tried traveling for a mercantile house. He was thus making his experience varied. About this time he united with the Congregational Church and began to study for the ministry. He studied theology about three years at Andover College. Mr. Gallaudet was very earnest and sincere. He desired to serve his Master acceptably.

He studied hard and wrote many letters for the newspapers. His name became well-known in New England. After he left Andover he was offered several churches in which to preach, but he did not accept any of them because his health was so poor. He did not seem to know just what to do. His opportunity had not yet come. He preached occasionally and traveled as much as he could for his health. Until 1817 there were no schools for the deaf and dumb in America. Only a few deaf persons had been taught to read and write. There were schools for the deaf in Germany, France, and England, but the people in America did not know anything about them. They were many deaf boys and girls in America. They were all very ignorant. They had no teachers to help them.

Mr. Gallaudet had several small brothers and sisters. Among their playmates were the children of Dr. Mason F. Cogswell. Dr. Cogswell was an eminent surgeon. He was a very popular man. He had a child named Alice, who was deaf. She was very bright, but she could not learn as fast as her sisters on account of her deafness. She often played with the Gallaudet children, for they were near neighbors. One day Mr. Gallaudet noticed Alice. He pitied her because she could not hear. He wished to teach her, so he tried to see what he could do. He first taught her the word "hat" then many other words and some sentences. When Mr. Gallaudet went back to college, Alice's parents, brothers and sisters kept on teaching her. She learned a great deal but not very fast, because they did not know how to teach deaf people very well then. Dr. Cogswell was a kind-hearted man. He thought very much about his daughter, Alice. He made inquiries and found there were many other deaf children in Connecticut. He thought it was a pity they should grow up in ignorance. He talked with other people about it and they decided to start a school for the deaf and dumb. Some kind men gave money to help them. They had heard about the schools for the deaf in England and France. They determined to send someone to England to learn about the schools there. They chose Mr. Gallaudet to go there and learn how to teach the deaf and dumb.

The English schools for the deaf were in the hands of a family named Braidwood. Mr. Gallaudet went to the Braidwoods and asked them to show him how to teach the deaf. The Braidwoods would not do it unless Mr. Gallaudet would give them much money. Mr. Gallaudet had no money to give them. He was very much disappointed. He spent several months trying to find out something about the Braidwood methods of teaching. He feared he would be unsuccessful. About this time Mr. Gallaudet heard that the Abbé Sicard was in London with two of his brightest pupils. He went to see them. He was delighted to see that the deaf could learn so much.

The Abbé Sicard invited him to visit his school in Paris and promised to help him all he could. Mr. Gallaudet was very glad and went to Paris. The Abbé Sicard was very kind and showed him how to teach the deaf and dumb. He remained there nearly a year, learning the signs and studying the methods of teaching. At last he was ready to return to America.

Laurent Clerc was one of the Abbé Sicard's assistants. He had also been his pupil for he was deaf. He had been a very bright boy and learned very fast. When he grew up Sicard appointed him to help him teach the deaf and dumb in his school in Paris. He was a good teacher and he assisted Mr. Gallaudet while he was in Paris. Mr. Gallaudet wished to take someone with him to America to help him start the new school. So he asked Mr. Clerc to go with him, and he consented. They landed in New York on August 9th, 1816.

While Mr. Gallaudet was in Europe, Dr. Cogswell and other friends had collected money and secured a charter for the "Connecticut Asylum." Several months were spent getting ready to open the new school. Finally on the 15th of April, 1817, the "Asylum" was opened for pupils. At first there were seven pupils. The first of these were Alice Cogswell, George H. Loring, and Wilson Whiton. Dr. Gallaudet's labors for the deaf were now fully begun and he labored incessantly for their good. Year after year new pupils were added and new teachers employed. The school grew rapidly and a new building was erected. The name of the institution was changed to the "American Asylum."

Dr. Gallaudet was principal of the "American Asylum" thirteen years. He worked very hard and taught a class himself all the time. He was not fairly treated by the board of directors but he did not complain. Besides working harder, he received less of a salary than did some of the teachers. Mr. Clerc received a higher salary than he.

Dr. Gallaudet was a small man. He was not strong but he had good control of his pupils. Some of them were large, rough boys, and some were bad. One day in the dining room Dr. Gallaudet stood up to say grace when a large boy seized a knife and rushed at him. He could not escape. He could not resist the large, strong boy. Dr. Gallaudet opened his bosom and told him to strike. The boy was instantly ashamed of himself and slunk away. Dr. Gallaudet loved the deaf and dumb and did all he could to help them. At last, after thirteen years' labor for the deaf, he retired from the "American Asylum" on account of poor health. He continued to reside in Hartford and visited the Institution often. In 1821 Dr. Gallaudet was married to Sophia Fowler who was deaf and who had been one of his first pupils. They had several children among whom are Dr. Edward Gallaudet, president of the National Deaf-Mute College, and Dr. Thomas Gallaudet, rector of St. Ann's Church for Deaf-Mutes in New York City. Mrs. Gallaudet lived many years after the death of her husband, and she was loved and honored by all who knew her.

After leaving the "Asylum" Dr. Gallaudet spent several years writing books for the young. He also wrote for the magazines. In 1838 he became chaplain in the Institution for the Insane at Hartford. He continued in this office until his death in 1851. In September of this year, he was confined to his home and to his bed most of the time. At last on the 10th, as he lay in his bed he thought he felt better. His daughter was with him. He said to her, "I will go to sleep." He slept in Jesus for he never waked again in this world.

Thomas Hopkins Gallaudet was the father of deaf-mute education in America. The deaf and dumb in the United States love to do honor to his memory. In 1854 they collected money and erected a monument to his memory in front of the Institution in Hartford. A bronze statue of Gallaudet, costing $10,000, was erected by the deaf on the grounds of the National Deaf-Mute College in Washington in 1889. It is right for the deaf to love him for he was a great and good man.

A Ring of Ill-Omen

Alphonso XII, king of Spain, had a splendid ring made. It was set with costly diamonds and pearls. He gave the ring to his cousin, Mercedes, the day they were betrothed. Mercedes lived but a short time after that. After the death of Mercedes the valuable ring was given to Alphonso's grandmother who died soon afterward. Then the king gave the ring to his sister, who died within a month. The ring was next worn by Christiene, the daughter of the Duke of Montpensier. In less than 100 days this lady was also dead. Alphonso then locked up the ring in his own casket and inside of a year the king himself was summoned by the grim reaper. The jewel was then placed around the neck of the statue of the Maid of Almadena, the patron saint of Madrid, where it still remains. It may be seen by everyone who passes. It is very valuable but no one dares to take it, so it is safe where it hangs in the public street.

Benjamin Franklin

B enjamin Franklin was one of the most distinguished men of this country. He was a great writer, a philosopher, and a patriot. When he was young he was honest and a hard worker. He studied very hard and read all the good books he could get.

Franklin was born in Boston, January 17th, 1706. His father was a soap boiler and candle maker. He was not rich and had to work hard to support a large family. Benjamin was the fifteenth child in the family. He learned to read while quite young. He was more delighted with a book than other children with toys. He attended school only two years. He learned very fast, however, and soon knew as much, and more than his brothers and sisters.

Benjamin did not read and study all the time when he was a child. He liked to play, too. He was very clever and often did amusing things and got into mischief like other boys. He was strong and active and an excellent swimmer.

At the age of ten, Franklin had to help his father in the soap and candle factory. He tended the store, filled the candle molds, and went on errands. He made himself useful but he did not like this kind of business. He wanted to do something that would help to improve his mind. He thought of running off to sea, but his father prevented it. At last he was apprenticed to learn the printing trade with his brother, James, who had a printing office in Boston. He liked printing because he could get more books and papers to read. He soon learned to write articles for the papers.

Benjamin and his brother, James, did not agree very well together, so they parted and Benjamin went to New York to get work. But in New York he could not get a job, so he concluded to go to Philadelphia. He had very little money, so he walked part of the way to Philadelphia. He tramped through rain and mud and was hungry sometimes. He did not give up but kept on. When he reached the "City of Brotherly Love," the first thing he did was to visit a baker's shop and buy some rolls. He carried a roll under each arm and one in his hand which he ate as he walked along the street. He did not care if the people smiled or laughed at him. One young girl, Dorothy Read, laughed heartily when she saw him. Franklin looked very funny. His clothes were splashed with mud and besides the rolls under his arms, his spare stockings and shirt were sticking out of his pockets. It was enough to make anybody laugh. In a few years, this same young lady became Franklin's wife and helped him in his business.

Franklin soon became the best printer in Philadephia. Governor Keith encouraged him to go to London to get a new press and types and promised to help him. When Franklin had reached London, he found that Keith had deceived him. He was without money or friends. He soon found employment in a printing office. Here he learned some new things about the business and earned enough money to go back to Philadelphia. He could make ink and cast types and engrave on type metal. He became a very useful man.

By and by Franklin had his own printing office and printed a newspaper, *The Pennsylvania Gazette*. It was the best newspaper in America at that time. He also studied hard and learned several languages. He could read French, Italian, Spanish, and Latin. He discovered that lightning was the same as electricity and invented the lightning rod. He became famous because he was wise and sensible.

Franklin was appointed to various public offices. He was elected to the Pennsylvania assembly for fourteen years. He was sent to England by the colonists to settle difficulties. After the War of the Revolution broke out, he was sent to France to persuade that country to assist the Americans. He was very successful.

Franklin also worked hard to improve the conditions of society in America. He organized the first police and first fire company in the colonies. He also founded the first library in this country. He started a hospital and a high school, which afterward became the University of Pennsylvania. He also organized the first society for the abolition of slavery.

On account of his many services to the colonists and his wisdom and sagacity, Benjamin Franklin became the most popular man in America, except Washington. He died on the 17th of April, 1790. He was mourned by the whole country and twenty thousand people attended his funeral.

Venice

Venice is a wonderful city in Italy on the Adriatic Sea. It is often called the "Queen of the Adriatic." It is a very old city and many years ago it was more powerful and more beautiful than it is now. It is full of interest and people from all over the world go to visit there, because it is so unlike other cities and because there are so many interesting things to be seen.

The city is built on eighty small islands, separated by wide and narrow channels. These channels are called canals. The houses cover the islands so completely as to make it appear that they were built up in the water. Nearly all the streets are canals. There are no rattling wagons and squeaky carts. People and goods are carried from place to place in boats called gondolas. These gondolas are very graceful and beautiful as they glide noiselessly along over the smooth water between the tall, stately houses. The houses open to the canals and the people step from their doors into the gondolas where they go any place. There are also narrow winding footpaths along the canals which are frequently crossed by graceful bridges.

One of the bridges in Venice is called the Rialto. It is a graceful arch of marble, one hundred and fifty-eight feet long. It is three hundred years old. It is lined on either side with little shops, where everything is sold. It is said the first newspaper ever published was sold on this bridge. The price of the paper was a coin, called a Gazetta. That is why, I suppose, so many newspapers are now called "Gazette."

St. Mark's is a famous cathedral, erected nearly eight hundred years ago. The stones, the marble and the timbers used in building it were brought from every country in Europe. In this wonderful church, repose the remains of St. Mark, so it is claimed. There are also four spiral columns here, said to have belonged to the temple of Solomon.

The Ducal Palace is a noted building. It is very large and wonderfully rich in ornament and fine workmanship. It was first built one thousand years ago, but has been destroyed five times. Each time it was rebuilt with more splendor than before. The governors of Venice hold their court in this building and in the rear, just across a narrow canal, is the gloomy prison with its dungeons and torture chambers. A bridge connects the Ducal Palace with the prison and is called "the bridge of sighs."

The Grand Canal is the fashionable avenue of Venice. It is very wide and about two miles long. Along this canal are the houses of the rich and many of them are beautiful marble palaces.

Memorial Address for Rev. John G. Brown, D. D.

This appeared in the November 1, 1915, issue of *The Western Pennsylvanian*.

In these days of contention and "war's alarm" we hear much of "preparedness for defense"—to be ready to fight our battles when they come our way. The battles of life in the times of peace are as strenuous as those of war and we are educated to be prepared to meet them. The deaf, more than any, need this preparedness.

What are our schools but for this purpose and schools for the deaf are their training camps. Every army, whether for war or peace, needs training because training breeds confidence, and experience increases efficiency. Therefore the more training and experience one obtains, the better fitted is he for the battle of life.

That country which has a trained soldiery and efficient fighting machine is better prepared for defense against the freebooter and the despoiler of liberty. "Millions for defense but not one cent for tribute" was a potent cry. In times of peace millions upon millions are explended for education and the training of our youth in order that they may make a success of life. Such is the right sort of preparedness, and every boy and girl needs it and it is their right. To be prepared is a duty to themselves, to the state and nation.

In centuries past the deaf were neglected blocks in the edifice human rights, only to be cast aside as fitting nowhere. Then came the master builders and discovered their niches when lo the edifice was complete and they no longer encumbered the earth. Education and training shape the blocks for every position from foundation to turret. All honor to these master builders!

The shaped block which has no enduring qualities is still worthless and the time spent on their shaping is wasted. So it is with him who receives his training and makes little use of it. Therefore, everyone is confronted with the duty of showing the metal he is made of. Much has been done for the deaf to lift them up to the plane of respectability. They climb higher or they may slide down. It is for them to choose which.

Dr. John G. Brown, like others before him, planted a seed and saw it grow and blossom into a great institution, the fruit of which is being garnered here at this reunion. It is no great stretch of fancy to suppose that he from the vantage on high sees and rejoices in the abundance and excellence of the fruitage which his vine has produced.

Let us review the planting of this institution and note the labors of its founder and builder.

It is meet that we are assembled here to do honor to our friend and benefactor, the founder of this magnificent institution, the Reverend John G. Brown, D. D. He loved the deaf and proved it by his numerous sacrifices and constant devotion to their interests. For forty-five years his greatest concern was the welfare of those sheltered by this institution as well as those who had left its protecting wall and gone forth to buffet with the storms of life.

He loved to be regarded as the grandfather of each and all of them as one bearing all the affection which that name implies. Until his last hours he loved to hear of their successes out in the bustling world of endeavor and grieved at any misfortune that crossed their path. He was happy to think that the school to which he had given the best part of his life and his most strenuous labor elevated them to a plane of prosperity and true happiness, and made them a part of the activities of human achievement. It is eminently fitting, therefore, that we think on these things and give him the meed, long delayed, of our loyalty to the institution which he founded and our love fostered and matured by the Alma Mater which he made possible.

Like other good men who dedicated their lives to uplift the deaf—men who blazed the way—he might have achieved great success in other walks of life, but the deaf appealed to him, he felt it was "a call" to special work, so he gave up a pastorate which promised a wide field of usefulness to devote his time and energies to their needs. He stood high in the estimation of his neighbors and in the councils of his church. For over fifty years he was a member of the Monongahela Presbystery and at one time its moderator. Members of this body gathered to do him honor on the fiftieth anniversary of his connection with the Presbystery. I mention this to show that he attained distinction and honors even while devoting the best part of his time and energies to the deaf who received the greatest and most lasting benefits from his efforts.

Dr. Brown believed in the biblical injunction, "Whatsoever thy hand findeth to do, do it with thy might." He thought that what was worth doing at all was worth doing well. He believed in practical employment for the young. He desired them to obtain as much industrial experience as was compatible with the means at hand.

These ideas of his were well exemplified in all he did for the school. He set out by looking into the future and visioned a grand institution that would hold rank with the best, although at that time he had but few deaf children in his control. He had nevertheless abundance of determination. With his small band of boys and girls he started the first day school in the United States and solicited support. It was not very long before he perceived that a day school could not produce the best educational and industrial results consequently it was promptly cast aside for a well-founded institution where pupils could be housed and received the care and attention that experienced and educated people could provide, although he knew the plan would entail great labor and worry on his part, for he was then practically alone.

With this object in view he interested practical businessmen and trained educators in the enterprise and soon had a Board of Trustees almost as enthusiastic as himself at his back.

He personally solicited contributions to carry on the school while at the same time he raised a fund of $50,000, conditioned on the legislature, for institution buildings.

When one of the finest buildings in the county, resultant of his work, was destroyed by fire in 1899, he repeated the performance while nearing his eightieth birthday, and behold, those fine substantial buildings you now enjoy are the fruits of his activities.

He, too, looking to the well-being of the deaf now and in the future, obtained the library fund from Mr. Carnegie. This fund still provides annual contribution of books to the library, and will so continue for future generations. The good that he has done lives after him.

Doubtless Dr. Brown made mistakes as most men do occasionally, but he was not the kind to cling to old and worn methods when he was once convinced there was something better to be had, nor did he give up or worry when any of his plans which he believed, to be the best were thwarted. He usually took the best he could get and made the most of it.

Dr. Brown believed the combined method of instruction was the best for the deaf as a whole, although he insisted that everyone capable of oral improvement should receive thorough instruction in that direction. Whatever was best for the individual he should have. So when the legislature demanded oral instruction as the price of its support, he made no complaint, but, with the assistance of his associates, set about devising plans whereby the best results possible under the new arrangement might be obtained. He was an optimist, not a pessimist.

But raising funds by subscription and looking to the growth of the institution educationally was not all of his work by any means. He had to meet opposition in the legislature and from other quarters. He fought for the rights of the school, that those sheltered by it should receive the greatest amount of benefit. Dr. Brown was always on the alert and used his powers to convince influential men of the justice of his cause. He took up the refutation of the claim that the school was educationally inferior. He stinted neither time nor labor to secure information that emphatically disproved the assertions of inferiority.

Dr. Brown was particularly gratified that he was spared to see the completion of the new buildings, the peer of any in the land, and to see that the school was entering upon a new era of usefulness. It was only then that he was content to retire and pass to others the lighter burden of upkeep.

These fine buildings are his monument. He cared not for bronze and marble but he rejoiced that he could leave behind him something that would be of lasting use to the deaf. It is for us who revere his memory to lift up his name in enduring bronze where those who pass by may observe and understand that we are not forgetful of our dues to our friend and benefactor.

Aaron Burr's Daughter

Aaron Burr was a noted figure in the United States early in its history. He was a noted lawyer and an ambitious and able man. He quarreled with Alexander Hamilton and killed him in a duel in 1804. Afterward Burr plotted against the government of the United States and was tried for treason. He was acquitted, but left the country and visited Europe.

Burr had but one child, a daughter. She was talented like her father, and very beautiful. She lived with her husband, a Mr. Alston, in Charleston, South Carolina. Her father, after a long visit to Europe, decided to return to America. He wrote to his daughter and asked her to meet him in New York. At that time there were no railroads. The only way to reach New York from Charleston was by stage or by ships. Burr's daughter decided to go by ship. Her husband did not accompany her. She took passage in a schooner for New York. She took with her her own portrait which she intended to present to her father, and a small dog. After she embarked at Charleston, she was never seen by her friends again. It was a long time before it was discovered what had become of her. It is now known that pirates captured the schooner in which she was, and murdered the crew and passengers by throwing them overboard. After robbing the vessel the pirates set it adrift and it was wrecked on the coast near Nags Head, North Carolina. Before the vessel went down, the people who lived on the coast rescued the picture and the dog. The picture is still preserved as a valuable relic of Aaron Burr and the tragic fate of his beautiful daughter.

Life Lessons

The Fox

A fox, which had been caught young, was kept as a pet. He was kept chained up in the yard and became very tame. The children played with him. The watch dog gamboled with him and the chickens and geese did not fear him but came up and pecked at his food without fear. The fox did not even growl at them. The mistress thought the fox was very pretty. She thought it was cruel to keep him chained up all the time. She thought it would be safe to let him loose. So she unbuckled the collar and let him go free. He was very glad to be unchained and frisked about. By and by the mistress heard a great noise and squalling among her geese and chickens. She ran out to see what was the matter. She saw the fox running away with her fattest pullet slung over his shoulder.

"You treacherous fox," shouted the woman, "I thought you were so good."

"Ah," said the fox, "I was good while I was chained, but now I am free."

Bad habits are like this fox. While we keep them chained and watch them, they give us no trouble. As soon as they are free they begin to rob us of our good qualities until we have a bad name. Beware of the little foxes, or bad habits.

The Boy and His Stomach

Once upon a time there was a little boy, who had a very fine stomach. He thought a great deal of his stomach. In fact, he was in love with it. The stomach was very greedy. The little boy gave his stomach many nice things, such as apples, oranges, bananas, grapes, nuts, cakes, figs, dates, and candy. He thought he was very kind to his stomach but he only spoiled it, because, after a while, it was never satisfied. It longed for something good all the time. The boy spent all his money for nice things for his stomach. His stomach kept on crying, "More, more," and the boy asked his mamma to help get him things for it. It troubled him very much but he could not refuse it. He let it have everything. By and by it became his master and was very troublesome. It gave him no peace. He could not study or think, because his stomach bothered him so much. When the boy was at work, his stomach troubled him and he had to stop and feed it, and give it good things to make it keep still.

So you see it does not pay to spoil a stomach. A spoiled stomach is like a spoiled child, very troublesome and annoying all the time.

The Lark and
the Young Ones

A lark had made her nest in a field of grain. She had young ones in the nest and the grain was almost ripe. The lark was fearful lest the owner would come and cut the grain before her birdlings were old enough to fly away. Every day when the lark went away to get food for her young ones, she strictly charged them to report to her what they might hear the farmer say about the grain. One morning the farmer and his son came to the field to look at the grain. The young larks heard the farmer say, "This grain is now ripe. Go to our friends and neighbors and tell them to come, help us reap it." When the old lark returned, the young ones, in much fear, reported what they had heard. They begged their mother to remove them at once. But the lark replied, "Do not fear. The grain will not be reaped tomorrow, if the owner depends on his friends and neighbors."

The next morning the farmer and his son came to the field but nobody came to help them. Then the father said to his son, "Our friends and neighbors have not come to help us. Now go to your uncles and cousins and tell them to come and help us reap our grain." Then the little larks were much frightened indeed. They told the old lark what they had heard and begged her to remove them quickly. But again the mother quieted them and said, "If the owner depends on his kinsfolk and relations the grain will not be cut tomorrow." She bade them be very careful what they heard the next time. The next morning the farmer and his son came to the field again but no one came to help them cut the grain. The man was disappointed. He said to his boy, "Get two good sickles and we will cut the grain ourselves tomorrow."

Again the young larks reported to the old lark, who replied, "Now indeed, we must move for when a man decides to do his own work it will be done." So the old lark moved her young ones to a place of safety and the farmer and his son cut down all the grain.

This story teaches us that we must not depend too much on others. It teaches us it is best to do our own work when we can. If we want to get rich we must work for ourselves. If we want wisdom we must study and think for ourselves.

The Grateful Dog

There was a little girl whose home was in Rome, Italy. She was about ten years old. She was a kind-hearted girl and always treated dumb animals kindly. Near her home, she often met a half-starved dog. This dog was not beautiful, nor was he clean, but the little girl pitied him because he had been treated unkindly and could not get enough to eat. She fed him crumbs from her lunch and caressed him. The dog seemed to appreciate her kindness.

One day the little girl was playing on a bridge which crossed the Tiber River. She was careless and fell from the bridge into the water. Many people saw her fall, but they could not help her. They ran about on the bridge. The policemen who saw her were afraid to go into the water to save the girl, and she would surely be drowned.

Suddenly a lean, yellow dog came barking to the river. He sprang into the water and swam out to the girl. He seized her dress and drew her to the shore. When he saw that she was safe he jumped about and barked loudly. He licked the girl's face and hands and showed that he was very glad. It was the dog which the little girl had fed and treated kindly. He remembered her and saved her life. He was a grateful dog.

It always pays to treat animals kindly.

Boys and Monkeys

There was a man who owned a large orange plantation in the South.

When the oranges became ripe, he employed many small boys to pick them, wrap them in tissue paper, and pack them in boxes.

One day a gentleman came to the grove with a monkey. It was very funny. It watched the boys pick oranges for awhile, then it scampered up a tree very quickly, picked an orange, brought it down, wrapped it in paper and put it in a box and then grimaced at the boys. The owner of the orchard was amused. He thought monkeys might make good pickers and so he bought a dozen monkeys and taught them to pick oranges. For awhile they did very well but by and by they became very careless and lazy. They had to be watched all the time or they would play or quarrel among themselves. The overseer of the plantation did not watch the boys at work. They had good sense and knew what to do after being told. The monkeys were mischievous and foolish.

When the overseer's back was turned, they would stop working. Sometimes they would throw oranges at each other and spoil the fruit, or they would chase one another up and down the trees and shake the oranges off and so bruise them. When the overseer held a stick in his hand and watched them, they would be very good but they could not be watched all the time. The longer that faithful boys remained in the orchard, the more useful they became for they learned all the time. When they grew up, some of them became orange growers themselves. But the longer the monkeys stayed, the more troublesome they became until at last, they were of no use and had to be sent away altogether. They learned nothing more than they knew at first.

Now some boys are like the monkeys. They learn a little but do not improve. They do not like to work and have to be watched and threatened like monkeys. They get into mischief and are quick to learn the foolish things they see other people do. In short, their minds do not grow and they soon become useless. Nobody wants to employ them and they are turned away and avoided. They are little better than chattering monkeys for they love to talk and talk about silly things all the time. A sensible boy likes to be busy and useful. He wants to learn useful things and improve his mind. His mind grows and he understands how to do things. He is not like the monkeys for he does better and better every day. Do not be a monkey, for it is only fit to be looked at and made fun of. Be a man.

The Miller and His Donkey

Once upon a time there was a miller. He lived long ago, but it does not matter where. He was not a very smart man but he was industrious and frugal. He worked hard in his mill and saved all he could. By and by he had saved enough to own a donkey. The animal was good and strong, and the miller thought he would sell it and get some money. There was a fair in the city some distance from the miller's home. He concluded to take the donkey there and sell it. One bright morning he started to the fair with the animal and his son. They did not ride. The father and son walked along the road and the donkey walked between them. As they trudged along the dusty road they met a company of gay, young men. They were laughing and talking. They noticed the miller and his son walking and leading the donkey. They laughed and made fun of the miller because neither he nor his son rode. They asked him why one of them did not get on and ride. Then the son quickly sprang upon the beast and rode while his father walked by the side.

A little further on they met some old merchants. They reproved the son who was riding. They called him a lazy lout because he did not walk and let his poor old father ride. Then the miller made the boy get off and he himself mounted the donkey. They traveled thus a little piece further and met a bevy of young girls. "What a shame!" exclaimed they, "that such a big, strong man should ride and make his poor boy walk." They asked the miller why he did not let his son ride. Then the miller thought he would please the girls and told the boy to get up behind him. So both rode the donkey and made a pretty heavy load for it.

Now they met many people on the road who noticed the two persons riding the little animal. They thought they were cruel and called them brutes. They said they ought to be ashamed of themselves. At last the miller and his son both got off. Then, thinking to please the people, they took up the donkey and carried it along on their shoulders. They thought the people would think they were kind. But now the people laughed and shouted. It was very funny to see the miller and his son carrying the donkey. They said the miller had a very funny pet. They wanted to know if he kept his pet in the parlor and if it was made of glass. The people asked many other funny questions. At last the miller and his son became angry and threw the donkey off their shoulders. The miller said he had tried to please everyone but could not. Now he would please himself and do as he thought proper. After that he got along very well and the people did not find fault with him any more.

This story teaches us that we cannot please everybody. We should do what is right and let people think as they please.

Two Kittens

Two cunning kittens, Jim Crow and Raven, shared the cozy home of a maiden lady. They had the sweetest milk to lap and the softest bed to sleep in behind the stove where it was warm. They were allowed the freedom of the house and could play among the downy cushions in the parlor. They were comfortable and happy when they did not quarrel, but I am sorry to say they often quarreled. They were greedy little things and each wanted the lion's share of everything.

It happened one cold, stormy day that Jim Crow had caught a nice fat mouse and Raven wanted a taste of it. Jim Crow would not give him any so they quarreled and spat at each other. Soon they unsheathed their sharp claws and began to scratch and fight. Their mistress saw the naughty kittens quarreling and with the broom swept them both out into the storm. The wind blew and the snow beat into their fur. Now they were glad to stop quarreling and huddle together in a corner of the porch. Soon they became very cold and mewed piteously. They thought of their cozy bed behind the stove. Perhaps they were sorry for having been so naughty. They mewed very loudly and scratched at the door. Their mistress heard them. She took pity on them and let them in. She thought they had been sufficiently punished for quarreling. Being cold and wet they crawled into their bed and lay close together like good friends. Soon they were fast asleep. They had forgotten all about the mouse which had caused all the trouble.

Boys and girls often quarrel and fight about little things and have to be punished to make them good again just like these kittens. It is best not to be covetous or angry.

Rudely Awakened

An ash wagon was standing in the street near the curb. There were some old boxes and barrels in the wagon. The owner was nowhere in sight. By and by a fat tramp came along. He noticed the wagon. He was tired and sleepy so he went and climbed upon the end of the wagon and sat down. He leaned back against the barrels and let his feet hang down outside. It was a comfortable seat and soon he went to sleep.

Two mischievous boys saw the tramp sleeping there. They also noticed that the wagon stood near a fireplug. They soon decided to have some fun. They procured a piece of strong rope and stole up to the wagon. One of them tied one end of the rope around the tramp's ankle while the other boy tied the other end around the fireplug. Then they ran and hid behind a house to see what would happen.

Pretty soon the owner of the wagon came back. He climbed into his seat, cracked his whip, and started his team. The tramp's leg being tied to the fireplug, he was dragged from the wagon. He fell on his back on the hard pavement and his dreams were rudely interrupted. When the naughty boys saw this, they danced with delight and ran away. They thought they had played a good joke on the tramp, but I think it was not very kind. The tramp learned that it is not safe to go to sleep in the public street.

Borrowed Plumes

Once there was a crow which lived with a company of other birds. Her feathers were plain and black. Her voice was harsh and coarse. She was awkward, but she was vain. She thought she had a fine head. The other birds did not like the crow very well. She thought it was because her feathers were so plain. She asked the other birds to lend her some feathers. The peacock gave her some long feathers for her tail. The goose gave her some white down for her neck. The hen gave her some for her wings. The turtledove gave her plumage for her back and the jay gave her one or two out of her crest for her head.

The silly crow stuck her borrowed feathers all over her body. Then she thought she was beautiful. She wanted all the other birds to see her, so she strutted about the yard. The other birds were very polite. They told her she was very pretty, but when her back was turned they made fun of her. They thought she was very silly. The crow sat upon a stump and tried to sing. Then all the other birds flapped their wings and ran away.

Now, some people are like this silly crow. They are not satisfied with their own clothes. They are vain and try to make other people think they are rich and pretty. They borrow their friends' things. Sometimes they borrow a hat, sometimes a coat, sometimes shoes, sometimes all they can get. Then they visit about and try to be smart. They simper and strut. Their friends laugh at them on account of their "borrowed plumes."

It is best to be contented with one's own things. If we act well we will be thought beautiful, and if we act silly we will be considered ugly, even if we have no fine clothes. "Handsome is what handsome does."

The Gentleman and the Banana Peel

A gentleman was walking along the street with a friend. All at once the latter stepped on a banana peel on the pavement. He slipped and fell down. His leg was badly broken. After this accident the gentleman could not bear the sight of a fruit peel on the sidewalk. He was afraid somebody would slip and be hurt like his friend. When he saw a peel on the pavement he always stopped and removed it. However busy he might be he never passed a fruit peel without sweeping it into the gutter. This had been his practice for many years. One day, not long since, he was walking along a crowded street. He saw a child in its mother's arms, drop a banana peel on the pavement. The gentleman dodged about among the people, seized the peel, and deposited it in the gutter. The people understood why he did it and were pleased with this act of thoughtfulness for the safety of others. They nodded approvingly. One lady wished to show her appreciation. She fumbled in her purse and took out a nickel. She pressed it into the gentleman's hand and said, "You did a kind act, sir, and should be rewarded." The gentleman was astonished and offended. He did not want to be paid for doing such things. He looked at the retreating lady and then at the coin. Then he pitched it into the street. The "street arabs" scrambled for it. Then they followed the gentleman along the street. They thought he was crazy and would throw more money away. They were disappointed, however. The gentleman had no more money to throw to them. It is right, though, to remove fruit peels from the sidewalks. It may save somebody much pain and suffering.

Absent-Minded

Once there was a noted artist. He could paint beautiful pictures and he loved his art. Whenever he found a nice smooth surface anywhere he liked to draw and paint pictures on it. One day his wife was sick and her back pained her very much. The doctor visited her and prescribed for her. He told her husband, the artist, to put iodine on her back with a brush. When the doctor was gone the artist got the iodine and a brush and proceeded to do as the doctor had directed. His wife's back was smooth and white. The artist imagined that it was a nice smooth canvas and began to paint a picture on it. He painted trees and flowers and other things. By and by his wife became impatient and asked him what he was doing so long. Then the artist came to himself and saw that he had painted a picture on his wife's back while he was dreaming. He told his wife what he had done by mistake and they both laughed heartily.

I think the laugh did his wife as much good as the iodine.

Animal Stories

Molly and the Canary

A lady had a pet canary bird of which she thought a great deal. She took very good care of it. The lady did not like cats because several times they had tried to catch her canary. She could not trust the cats and did not keep any. One day some boys passed her house, carrying a kitten. She heard them talking and learned they were going to drown it. The lady was kind-hearted and did not like to think of the kitten being drowned. She called the boys to her and offered to keep the kitten. They said another lady would give them five cents to drown it. So she gave the boys five cents for the kitten and saved it from a watery grave. She called it Molly. She took good care of it and as it grew up she noticed that the canary and Molly were very friendly. The kitten never tried to catch the bird. By and by the lady let the bird out in the room with the cat, while she was present. The bird would often perch upon Molly's back or head without fear. They became more and more friendly, so at last their mistress often left them alone in the room together. She trusted Molly.

One day the lady went away to call on a neighbor and left the canary and the cat alone in the room. When she came home she saw that there was something wrong. When she opened the door she discovered Molly on the mantel with the bird in her mouth. At first she thought she had killed her dear little bird. She seized a cane and was going to strike Molly with it but just then a strange yellow cat sprang through the open window and ran away. Then the lady understood why Molly had seized the bird and got upon the mantel. She had saved it from the strange cat.

As soon as the strange cat had gone Molly let the canary go and went up to her mistress to be petted. The bird was not hurt the least bit, and the lady was very grateful to her cat for saving it. After this Molly always took care of the bird and the lady loved them both very much.

Fight with an Owl

A farmer, named Cross, lived in Oklahoma. One day he saw an owl on the roof of his barn. He got his gun and fired at the bird, knocking it off the roof. He went to pick it up but it was not dead. The shot had broken its wing and this made it furious. When the farmer approached, the wounded bird flew into his face and began to fight furiously. Again and again it flew into his face. It tore and scratched the skin with its beak and sharp claws. Mr. Cross was compelled to flee to save himself. As he turned he stumbled and fell. The owl instantly pounced upon him.

Then the farmer's shepherd dog rushed to the rescue. The bird then flew at the dog and they fought fiercely. While they were fighting, the farmer jumped up, ran into the barn, got a spade and returned to the fight. He dealt the bird several hard blows on the head with the spade and stunned it. It fell on the ground and it took several more blows to kill it.

The dog was badly injured about the head and neck and one eye was torn out. The owl measured four feet across the wings and its head was as large as a baby's.

The Bird and the Snake

A gentleman had a beautiful songbird. It could sing very sweetly and the gentleman loved to hear it. He kept it in a pretty cage and fed it with seeds. One day he hung the cage near an open window and went away. There was a large grape vine growing at the side of the house. It reached to the window. A large snake was crawling about the yard for something to eat. It heard the bird singing. It climbed up the grape vine to the window. It crept into the cage. It caught the bird and swallowed it. After it had swallowed the bird it could not get out of the cage. The gentleman came home. He went to the cage and saw the snake there. He knew it had eaten his dear little bird. He was very sorry. He killed the snake.

"Hiram's Cow"

Hiram was a country boy. He was about thirteen years old. He was a sensible boy and liked to work. He had to drive his father's cows to and from the pasture every day. The pasture was a good piece from the house, near the woods.

One day Hiram started after the cows. When he was about half-way through the pasture he saw all the cows running towards him. They were bellowing and seemed to be frightened. Hiram wondered what could be wrong. He quickly hid behind a tree to see what the cows would do. The cows ran past one after another. The old bell cow came last and just ahead of her was a bear. The bear had come out of the woods and frightened the cows.

After the cows had all passed, Hiram ran after them. The cows and the bear all ran into the barnyard. Hiram closed the gate and fastened it. The cows, then, began to chase and hook at the bear. They all ran round and round the yard. It happened that the upper half of the barn door was open. So the bear jumped through into the barn and the cows could not follow it. Then Hiram ran and closed the barn door and the bear was imprisoned.

After that Hiram ran into the house and told the folks that he had a bear in the barn. They all ran out to see it. They peeped through the cracks at it. Hiram's little sister had never seen a bear before and did not know what it was. She said it was "Hiram's new cow." It was a young bear and Hiram kept it in the barn until it became tame. Then he let it out and it would follow him about like a dog. He called it Shaggy Coat but the folks usually called it "Hiram's cow."

The Tiger's Bath

There was a French animal trainer named Pezon. He had a large number of wild animals in cages. Some of these he had tamed and others were untamed. Pezon traveled about to exhibit his animals to the people. One time he was at Moscow with his menagerie. It was necessary for him to get somebody to clean the cages. He found a bright looking Cossack and hired him to do the work. The Cossack did not understand a word of French so Pezon made signs and acted with a broom, sponge and water bucket to show him how to clean the cages. The Cossack smiled and nodded. He seemed to understand so Pezon left him to attend to the job the next morning.

In the morning the Cossack came with a broom, sponge, and a bucket of water. He opened the first cage he came to and stepped in. The cage happened to be occupied by a fine but untamed tiger. It lay on the floor of the cage fast asleep but when it heard the noise of the shutting of the door, it awoke. It raised its head and looked curiously at the Cossack.

Just as the man entered the cage, Pezon came in and saw him. He expected to see the tiger tear the foolish man to pieces. He stood spellbound and watched the two in the cage. The tiger did not move. The Cossack did not know he was in any danger. He soused his sponge into the bucket of water and walked up to the tiger. He took the sponge out of the water and began to wash the tiger. The water was cool and the tiger seemed to like it. The creature began to purr. It stretched out its paws, rolled over on its back and allowed the man to sponge it all over. The Cossack scrubbed with might and main. All the time Pezon stood with his eyes wide open, watching the pair. At last the bath was done and the Cossack coolly left the cage. It was a very lucky escape.

Pezon was angry with the man because he did not understand him. He wanted him to scrub the cages but the Cossack thought he wanted him to bathe the animals. Signs and pantomime are not always plain, as this story shows.

A Huntress

Mrs. Amelia Fisher lived in California. She was brave and could use a rifle as well as any man. She often went out hunting and was usually very successful.

One day she was out hunting. She tramped about the mountain side until late in the afternoon. Game was scarce and she had secured nothing. Just as she concluded to go home a large buck came in sight. She fired at the animal and gave it a mortal wound. It then disappeared among some bushes. The huntress followed the trail of blood which led into an open space. Here she saw a sight that startled her. In the middle of the space lay the buck and a huge panther was feasting on his carcass. She did not expect to find such fierce game. In a moment her fear had disappeared and she advanced boldly toward the robber of her prey. When she was near enough she leveled her rifle and fired at the panther. Her aim was true and the beast lay dead beside the buck.

Having killed the panther, the woman's nerves gave way and she fell fainting on the ground. Here she lay two days without food or shelter and was found by a party of friends who had been out looking for her.

The Stork and the Dog

A large stork lived in the park. A stork is a large queer-looking bird. It has very long legs and a long bill. One day a small dog came into the park. He came near the stork. Just then somebody threw an apple on the grass. The dog wanted to play with the apple and the stork wanted to eat it. They both ran after it. The stork reached it first and picked it up. He held it in his bill and the dog ran about and barked at the stork. The stork could not swallow the apple so he put it down and jabbed it with his bill. The dog ran and took the apple away from the stork. But the stork ran after the dog and made him drop the apple. The stork got it again. He could not eat it because when he put it down, the dog would run for it. Many people watched the dog and the stork. They were much amused.

The Lion and the Spaniel

There is a place in London called the Tower. Many years ago wild animals were kept in cages in a part of the Tower. People could go there and see them. At one time they had a lion in the Tower. He was very large and fierce and a great many people wanted to see him. They had to pay a small fee to see the king of the forest. If any one could not pay the fee he might bring a live cat or dog to feed to the lion. A good many live animals had thus been given to the lion and he had always torn them in pieces instantly and devoured them.

Well, one day a small boy wanted to see the lion but he had no money. He captured a pretty little spaniel on the street and carried it to the lion. The dog was thrown into the cage. It shrunk back into the corner, whined pitiously, and trembled. The lion was not hungry. He walked up to the spaniel and smelled at it. He crouched and played with it.

The keeper, seeing this, brought a mess of food and put it into the cage. The lion would not eat it. He wanted the dog to eat. By and by the dog began to eat, then the lion ate also. So they ate together and had a very friendly dinner. After that the dog and the lion were great friends and lived together happily. The lion was very kind and gentle and the spaniel was very bold and saucy. Often the dog would bark, pull the lion's mane and bite his ears, but the lordly animal would never be cross or hurt the dog.

A gentleman who had lost the spaniel found him with the lion. He claimed his dog and wanted to take him away. The keeper told him he might take the spaniel if he could but he dared not go into the cage, so he had to leave his dog there. The great lion and the little spaniel lived together a long time but at last the dog took sick and died. The lion did not understand it. He thought his little friend was sleeping.

But as the dog did not wake up the lion began to feel uneasy. He smelled at the carcass of the dog. He rolled it over with his paw and brought it food. He seemed to be in great distress and could often utter a prolonged roar. They tried to take the carcass from the cage but the lion would become furious and fly at them violently. The keeper was afraid that the cage would break, so they had to let the body of the dog remain. The lion would eat no food. He lay down by the body of his friend and moaned. At last the lion died, it seemed, of a broken heart. The spaniel and the lion were buried together in one grave.

Saved by Sheep

In the far west, snow storms often occur. Sometimes the snow falls so fast and thick that people cannot see far through it. Sometimes people get lost in the snow and freeze to death. Houses are far apart and there is nothing to guide one through the snow.

Little Nellie Logan lived in Idaho. She was about six years old. She attended school which was some distance from her home. On Monday, Nov. 14, 1892, Nellie started to school. She carried her dinner in a small lunch basket and her little dog accompanied her. Soon after she left home it began to snow very hard. The wind blew and soon the path was covered up. Nellie could not see far through the fast-falling snow and by and by lost her way.

By noon she had not reached the schoolhouse and her friends knew she was lost in the snow. A search for her was commenced at once. Parties of white men and Indians wandered over the snow-clad hills day and night hoping to find her. Her friends did not expect to find her alive, but they hoped to find her body. On Wednesday her little dog was found frozen stiff. Still the search for Nellie was continued. At last, on Saturday, the little wanderer was found alive and well, but very weak.

She was found with a dozen fleecy sheep in an old stock shed. She had snuggled in among the sheep and so escaped death by freezing. Nellie told her friends that on Monday, while she was wandering about in the snow, she had heard the sheep bleating and went to them. Her friends were glad, indeed, to find her alive. They took good care of her and soon she got strong and hearty again. It was a wonderful escape.

Elenore and Nero

Aunt Elsie had a little niece named Elenore. She was over two years old and had just begun to lisp and prattle. She could say many cute things and all her uncles and aunts loved her very much. They thought a great deal of her.

At Christmas time Aunt Elsie went out to her old home in the country to spend Christmas. The folks prepared to have a good time with roast turkey, plum pudding, pumpkin and mince pies and doughnuts. They also trimmed a tree in the parlor. Little Elenore was there. She was the pet of every one.

At this house there was a large dog named Nero. He was a mastiff, very large and strong. He was cross sometimes and would not let the folks tease him. Nero seemed to like little Elenore very much. She would pull his tail or his fur and he was never cross. She could ride on his back and sleep with her head on his shaggy back. Nero would follow Elenore all about the house and let no one hurt her. He seemed to think she needed him to watch her.

Well, the day before Christmas, while they were trimming the tree, they needed more green boughs and moss. They sent Aunt Elsie to the woods for them. It was not far to the woods, so she decided to take Elenore with her in her baby carriage. They wrapped the baby up warm with cloaks and shawls. As they started away, Nero came and wanted to go with them, but Aunt Elsie stamped her foot and told him to stay at home. Nero hung down his head and went into the house.

When they reached the woods, Aunt Elsie cut a lot of green boughs and collected some moss. They were soon ready to go back to the house. Then auntie thought of the mountain tea which grew near that place. She concluded to go and pick some for Elenore. She left the baby in the carriage and hastened away among the trees to a place where the berries grew. She gathered a handful of the green leaves and bright berries and hurried back. She had been gone about ten minutes, but when she got back the carriage was empty. Elenore was gone. She was very much frightened. She looked all around and called, "Elenore, Elenore," but received no answer. She ran here and there through the woods but she could not find the baby. She was in despair. It was getting late so she hurried back to the house to tell her friends that Elenore was lost in the woods. When she reached the house she was out of breath and so frightened that she could not speak. She pointed at the empty carriage to make them understand that Elenore was lost. Elenore's mamma took Aunt Elsie by the arm and led her into the parlor.

Everybody was happy except Aunt Elsie. She looked at the tree, which they were trimming, and at the happy faces of her friends. Then she saw—what do you think? Why, Elenore and Nero, both fast asleep on the rug before the fire! She thought the child was lost, and there she was, safe at home! She was very glad indeed. Nero had followed them to the woods, and while Aunt Elsie was away, stole the child out of the carriage and brought her home. Was he not a sly old dog?

The Monkey and the Sugar

Monkeys, like children, are fond of sweet things. They are particularly fond of sugar and bon-bons. Once a pet monkey was given a bottle with a hard lump of sugar in it. The bottle was tightly corked so he could not pull it out. The monkey could see the sugar through the glass and wished very much to get it. He shook the bottle and rolled it on the floor but the sugar would not come out. Then he tried the cork. He could not get that out either. The sugar seemed to be very near his reach but he could not get it. He began to act very funny and the people were much amused to see him try to get the sugar. Sometimes he would sit up with folded arms and look longingly at the sugar. Then he would clasp the bottle in his arms and hug it and bite at the sugar through the glass. At other times he would lie down and fondle the bottle with his hands. Then he would sit up and look very sad because he could not get the sweets. He tried many ways to get the sugar and was very amusing. He kept on trying.

It happened his mistress had a jar of pickles on the table. By some means it was knocked off the table. It fell with a crash on the floor and was broken in pieces. The pickles rolled out on the floor. The monkey witnessed this accident. Instantly he seized the bottle containing the sugar and jumped up on his perch. He threw the bottle to the floor and it was broken. The sugar rolled out and the monkey seized it and began to munch it with much pleasure. He grimaced and winked at the people. He seemed to say, "Ah! I got it at last!" I think he deserved it after trying so hard.

The Toad, The Snake, and the Tramp

A toad lived in a pile of loose stones near a stone-bridge. It often hopped out among the weeds and on the road. It caught flies, bugs, and worms to eat. One day it was sunning itself on a flat stone near the railroad. By chance a snake came along that way, looking for its dinner. It spied the toad. It crept up and caught it. It swallowed it whole. The snake did not go away but coiled up and lay there in the sun. By and by a tramp came along, walking with a cane. He saw the snake and killed it with his stick. Then the tramp walked on the railroad and a locomotive ran over and killed him. The toad killed the bug. The snake killed the toad. The tramp killed the snake. And the locomotive killed the tramp. So that was the end of them.

Retellings

Lady Jane of Lorn

Lady Jane of Lorn lived long, long ago among the hills of Scotland. She was beautiful and good. She had many lovers. One of them was a wealthy chieftain named Maclean. Lady Jane did not love him. She loved another man who was good, but poor. Her father, brothers and friends did not want her to marry the poor man. They made her take Maclean for her husband because he was rich and powerful. They were proud people and did not want a poor relation. Lady Jane was not happy and by and by Maclean became tired of his wife. He wanted to get rid of her. So he contrived to have her placed upon a large rock near the seashore and left her there alone. He knew when the tide came in the water would cover the rock and drown his wife. The next day he thought that she was dead. He prepared a coffin and placed stones and dirt in it. Then he called Lady Jane's friends and relations to come to the funeral. He told them that Lady Jane had been sick and died. He pretended to be very sorry and wept. The friends of Lady Jane said nothing. They wrapped their plaids about them and silently followed the coffin to the grave.

Now it happened that Lady Jane was discovered on the rock by the sea before the tide came in and rescued. She went to her father's house and told them about the cruel Maclean. So when Maclean told them that Lady Jane was dead they knew that he lied. They pretended to believe him until they reached the grave.

Maclean asked them why they were so silent and why they kept their plaids wrapped around them. Suddenly each one opened his plaid and each had a long dagger in his hand. Maclean was very frightened and turned very pale. Lady Jane's kinsmen demanded that the coffin be opened. Then they saw the stones and dirt and asked Maclean why he had deceived them. He could say nothing but threw himself upon his knees before them and begged them to spare his life. They stabbed him with their daggers and killed him there. They put his body into the empty coffin and buried him in the grave he had meant for his wife. He was punished for his cruelty and treachery.

Echo

Long, long ago, it is said, Echo was a beautiful maiden but not very wise.

Stories of long ago tell us about Diana, who was a goddess and lived in the forests and dells. Echo also lived among the hills and woods and was a favorite of Diana. They were often seen together, for wherever Diana went, Echo was sure to follow.

Now, Echo was very loquacious. That is, she loved to talk. Her tongue never seemed to get weary. She was young and silly, and by and by she fell into the bad habit of talking back at people. When she was in the company with older and wiser persons and discussing grave matters, Miss Echo would insist on having the last word. She also tattled and often changed the words that she had heard. So it is no wonder, she was disliked on account of her bad habits.

Juno, it is said, was the chief of the goddesses. One time Echo heard Juno say something very nice and reported her wrong. It made the goddess very angry and she determined to punish the saucy maid. She declared that Echo, on account of her folly, should no longer talk like other people. She should never again say anything first herself, but all she should say would be in reply to others or to repeat what others said. This was a terrible punishment for poor Echo, for she was lively and loved to talk, nevertheless she could not escape. Soon after this Echo met one, Narcissus, whom she wished very much to please. She tried again and again to speak to him but to her sorrow, she found that she was mute. She could not utter a word. At another time, Narcissus, seeing Echo was very beautiful, spoke to her, but she could only repeat his words and seemed to mock him, so he became very angry and left her. He never spoke to her again.

Poor Echo wondered about the dells on the mountain sides. She was very sad and pined away in her sorrow. She grew smaller and smaller until at last, her form disappeared entirely. Her voice however was immortal and could not die. It is living still and often people can hear the voice of Echo. When they shout they can hear the voice repeating their words and when they laugh Echo will laugh back at them. Often she repeats the words again and again and makes the mountain sides fairly ring with music and strange sounds. When people are tempted to tattle to tattle and gossip they should remember the story of Echo, for, like her, they might be punished for what they say.

Arachne

Long ago people believed there were many gods and goddesses. Minerva was the goddess of all liberal arts. This included spinning, weaving, sewing, and embroidery. None could spin, weave, sew or embroider as well and skillfully as Minerva.

There was a young woman named Arachne, the daughter of a dyer. She learned to sew and embroider when she was very young and became skillful. Her friends flattered her and said that Minerva, the goddess, must have been her teacher. Arachne denied this and said she learned herself without a teacher. She was very vain of her needlework. She boasted that she could sew and embroider as well as the goddess. She even challenged Minerva to a trial of skill.

Now, in those days it was considered very wicked for anyone to compete with the gods and goddesses and they were usually severely punished for so doing. Arachne knew all this but she was willing to suffer if she failed to do better work than Minerva.

Minerva heard of Arachne's boastings and was much displeased. She assumed the form of an old woman and went to see the foolish maiden. She warned her not to compete with the goddess. Arachne was angry and told the old woman to mind her own business. She said she was not afraid of the goddess. Then Minerva threw off her disguise and the company knew it was the goddess herself. All bowed down before her. Arachne, alone, stood defiant. She still resolved to compete with the goddess. The contest began at once. Each put up her piece of embroidery and began to work on the designs. Both worked very fast. The skillful fingers moved rapidly over the surface of the web. With her needle Minerva wrought some beautiful scenes of the gods and goddesses. All her work was pure and noble. She also embroidered scenes where mortals contested with the gods and were punished. She hoped Arachne would give up before it was too late.

Arachne wrought in her web pictures to show the weakness and foolishness of the gods and goddesses. When Minerva saw these pictures of the presumptious maid, she was very angry. She struck the embroidery with a shuttle and tore it from the frame. She then touched Arachne on the forehead and caused her to feel her folly and guilt. Arachne could not endure this, so she went and hanged herself. Minerva pitied her. She told her, she should live, but she and all her descendants should continue to hang by a thread forever. Then she sprinkled the juice of a plant over her, and immediately Arachne's form began to change. Her body shrunk up. Her head grew small. Her fingers grew to her sides and served as legs. She continued to spin but the threads were made out of her own body. With these she suspended herself and made webs in the air. Alas, poor Arachne! she had been changed into a spider.

Vanlander and Amilias

Vanlander was a famous smith. He was the Scandinivian Vulcan. Vanlander was at the court of King Nidung. His fame as a smith became known there. This caused the king's smith, Amilias, to become jealous of Vanlander. He wanted the people to think him the best smith in the kingdom. Accordingly he challenged Vanlander to a trial of skill. Amilias was to make a suit of armor and Vanlander a sword. If Vanlander's sword could cut through Amilias's armor then Amilias's life should be forfeited to Vanlander. But if Vanlander's sword could not pierce the armor, then Vanlander's life should be forfeited to Amilias. Twelve months were allowed for the trial.

Amilias worked at his armor the whole twelve months but Vanlander did not begin his task until two months before the trial. Then he went to his smithy and forged a beautiful sword which was very large and heavy. He showed it to the king. The king admired its beauty. To test the sword, Vanlander took a cushion, filled with wool, one foot thick. He put this cushion in a stream and allowed it to float down against the edge of the sword. The sword cut the cushion in two. The sword cut it in two. The king thought it was a remarkable sword but Vanlander did not think it was good enough. He took it back to his smithy and filed it all up. He made a new sword out of the filings. This he took to the king. They tried the new word as before but this time the cushion was two feet thick. The sword cut it in two easily. King Nidung thought the sword was surely good enough now but Vanlander was not satisfied. He returned to his smithy and again filed down the sword and made a new one. This time it was the proper size. It was polished and adorned with jewels. He took it to the king who admired its beauty and workmanship. They took it to the river and now they had a cushion three feet thick. This cushion floated down against the edge of the sword and was cut in two without stopping a moment. Vanlander was now satisfied.

The day for the test arrived. Amilias put on his new armor. It was made of double plates of steel. He felt sure Vanlander's sword could not pierce it. Amilias seated himself in a chair before the king and his court. He bade Vanlander to do his best. Vanlander took his sword and stood behind his rival. He lifted the sword and smote Amilias on the helmet with all his might. Then he asked Amilias if he felt anything. He said he felt as if cold water was running through him. "Shake yourself," said Vanlander. Amilias did so and his head felt asunder. The terrible sword had cleft both the armor and his head to the chin. So Vanlander won the contest with his wonderful sword.

The Lady of the Lawn

The lady of the lawn was very pretty. She was tall and graceful. She wore a beautiful green dress, with sleeves which were
very large and spreading. They were covered with fine lines and
net-work. In fact, her sleeves were large enough for wings. The
dress was fastened with knots of emerald and sapphire bows. Her
eyes were large and lustrous. Her feet were small and encased in
dainty bootees. Indeed, she was always well and tastefully dressed
and scrupulously clean. She was, as you see, a very interesting little
thing. The lady was a musician, too, and her songs were often
heard by her neighbors.

This interesting little lady lived on a most lovely lawn at the edge
of a shady wood. Her home was protected by tall ferns and bam-
boos and fragrant flowers adorned the paths through her yard and
gardens. Her food consisted of the tenderest parts of maize and
various grains. She was also passionately fond of "greens." In fact
she was strictly a vegetarian and she disdained the taste of meat of
any kind. She always had the appearance of being plump and
sweet, so I suppose, she did not need animal food.

Now, I suppose you are very anxious to know who this interesting little lady was. Well, her name was Miss Katy-Did. She seemed
to be very proud of her name too for often she was heard out on the
lawn repeating in sharp tones. "Katy-Did," "Katy-Did," "Katy-Did."

Issa

Tibet is in Asia, north of India. The people who live there are Buddhists. They worship Buddha, who lived and taught the people long before Jesus came to be our Saviour. The priests of Buddha are called Llamas. They live in the temples of Buddha and also in monasteries.

Not long ago a noted Russian traveler, named Nicholas Natovich, was traveling in the mountains of Tibet. One day he had the misfortune to break his leg. He was carried to a Buddhist monastery and taken care of by the Llama in charge. While the traveller was at the monastery he learned that they had a very old story, in their own language of the life of Christ. This was the Buddhist account of Jesus. Mr. Natovich tried very hard to buy the manuscript but the Llama would not sell at any price. He, however, allowed Mr. Natovich to have a translation of it. The Buddhists call Christ the prophet Issa, and this is the way they tell the story:

Issa was born of Israeli parents who were poor but very pious. They were unfortunate in life but they never doubted God's goodness. From his childhood Issa preached *one* God. He never married. At the age of thirteen, he fled from his father's house and went with some merchants to Sindah. When he was fourteen years old, he lived with the Arians in India. The people were Brahmins. They worshipped Para Brahma. Issa rebuked them and told them that their god Brahmin and their holy book Veda were not divine. After this Issa learned the Pali language and all the mysteries of Buddhism. Then he went westward and preached against idols. He was twenty-nine years old when he returned to Judea. He began to preach and became very popular. The people liked him. Pontius Pilate, the ruler of Judea, was alarmed. Pilate commanded the priests and wise men to try Issa. The court examined Issa and decided that he was innocent of any wrong.

Issa continued to preach to the people. He told them to obey Caesar and to respect all womankind. Pilate set spies to watch Issa. The spies reported that great multitudes assembled to hear him preach. The governor was alarmed. He thought Issa was trying to become ruler of Judea in his place. So Pilate caused him to be put in prison and tortured. He also had him tried before the Sanhedrim, the Jewish court. Two thieves betrayed Issa and told lies about him in order to please Pilate. One of the thieves said that Issa claimed to be the king of Israel. Issa blessed this man and told him he should be forgiven because his words came not from the heart. Issa then told Pilate he was able to condemn an innocent man without bribing thieves to lie. This made Pilate very angry and he ordered that Issa be put to death on the cross.

The judges told Pilate that Issa was innocent and it was a great sin to condemn him. Then the priests and wise men went out and washed their hands in a holy vessel, saying, "We are innocent of the death of a just man." Issa and the two thieves were crucified. They were placed in their tombs, but on the third day Issa's sepulchre was found to be open and empty.

And this is the story of Christ as told by the Buddhists in Tibet.

People Stories

The Ugly Aunt

Long ago there was a little girl whose parents were dead and who had no brothers and sisters. This poor orphan was left all alone without friends to take care of her. She had no relations. Her name was Geraldine. She was very beautiful and she was always anxious to learn and willing to work. This was well for she had to earn her own living.

In that country there was a fine palace where lived a powerful queen. To this palace Geraldine went to get a place as maid to the queen. Now when the queen saw her she loved her for her beauty, and chose her to wait on her, and always be near her. The queen did not mind how poor she was. Geraldine was very happy for she liked to work for the queen and tried to please her.

At last there was trouble. The other maids in the palace of the queen were jealous of Geraldine. They hated her because the queen loved her best and had chosen her to be her favorite. They annoyed her and teased her. They tried to make her angry but she was very patient. Finally they thought how they could injure her. The queen loved to spin. She thought no one could spin as fast or as fine as she. So those wicked maids told the queen that Geraldine had boasted that she could spin a pound of flax all in one day. This was not true but the queen did not know it. She thought Geraldine was very boastful. So she put her in a room all by herself and gave her a spinning wheel and a pound of flax. She bade her show how well she could spin, then left her alone.

Poor Geraldine was very much troubled. Her mother had never taught her how to spin and she was in despair. She sat down and cried for she knew not what to do. Just then the door opened and a queer looking woman came in. She was very old and ugly with a long nose. She asked the maid why she cried and she told her about the flax which she could not spin. Then the old woman told her that she would spin the flax and she should go to bed, if on her wedding day she would call her *aunt*. Geraldine promised. Then the woman spun the flax very fast and soon finished it all. After that she went away.

In the evening the queen came into the room to see how her maid had got along with her task. She was very much surprised to see that the flax was all spun, and how fine and even the thread was. She embraced Geraldine and kissed her. She said she was very smart to spin so well, and that she should wed her son, the prince.

So there was a grand wedding at the palace and Geraldine became a princess. There was a fine wedding feast and many guests were at the table. While they were eating and laughing the door flew open and a funny old woman came bouncing in. The guests were astonished. The woman curtesied to all and said to the princess, "Good evening, gentle lady." Geraldine replied, "Good evening, *aunt*." The prince was much surprised to hear his bride call this ugly, wrinkled woman her aunt. He made room at the table and politely invited her to sit by him at the feast. While he ate, the prince could not help wondering why this old woman had such a long nose. At last he asked her how her nose happened to be so long. She answered, "It was spinning in my girlhood that made my nose so long." The prince stared. Then he declared before all his guests that his bride, the beautiful Geraldine, should never spin again, for he did not want her to spoil her beauty, and become ugly with a long nose like her aunt. So Geraldine was never asked to spin again and lived happily with the prince.

The Maid of the Inn

An inn is a house where travellers stop to get their meals and sometimes stay overnight. Many years ago there were many inns in England and many travellers stopped at them to drink and eat. At one of these inns, there was a young girl named Mary. She waited on the guests and brought them whatever they wanted. She was the maid of the inn. She was beautiful and good. She was always cheerful and tried to please everybody. She often prayed to God and she knew he would take care of her. So she was never afraid of the dark. Everybody liked her and many praised her. They knew that she was a true, good girl. By and by she had a lover. His name was Richard. Soon they were to be married. Now Mary's friends did not like Richard because he was always idle and did not like to work. They thought Mary would be very unhappy if she married him.

Well, one night it was very stormy. The wind blew hard and made the trees creak and groan. There were two guests at the inn. They were sitting by a table, smoking and talking about the weather. They thought it was a terrible night.

A short distance from the inn there was an old ruined abbey. There were many dark empty rooms and dark corners about the ruins. One of the men said he knew no one would dare to go to the old abbey during such a stormy night. The other man said he knew Mary, the maid of the inn, would not be afraid. The first man laughed and said he knew Mary would be frightened by a white cow if she saw one.

Then they called Mary and asked her if she would go alone to the old abbey. She said she would go and that she was not afraid. So it was agreed that she should bring a bunch of elder, which grew in the middle of the ruins to prove that she had been there. Then Mary put on her hood and shawl and started out. The wind blew furiously and soon she shivered with the cold. In a short time she reached the ruins and made her way over the piles of stones and through the dark rooms. The wind roared through the ruins but Mary was not afraid. At last she reached the clump of elder and quickly picked a bunch to take back with her. Just then she was startled by hearing voices nearby. Now she began to be frightened. In a little while the wind ceased to blow hard and she heard footsteps approaching. She trembled with fear but she quickly hid behind a broken column. She peeped from behind her hiding place and saw two men carrying a corpse between them. All at once the wind blew hard again and the hat of one of the men was blown from his head and rolled to Mary's feet. Mary thought she would surely be discovered and her heart beat fast. The men, however, were very anxious to conceal the dead body which they bore, so the man did not follow his hat and soon they passed on.

When the men had gone Mary seized the hat and ran very fast out of the ruins. She rushed breathless into the inn and fell on the floor. She could not speak because she was so frightened. Presently she noticed the hat which she had brought with her. Then she screamed and fainted away for she recognized her lover, Richard's hat. She knew, then, that he was a murderer.

Richard was caught, tried in court before a judge, and sentenced to be hanged.

Poor Mary! Her mind became weak and she soon lost her reason. She wandered about the village and never smiled again. Her clothes became ragged and torn but she did not notice them. Everybody felt sorry for her but they could not help her. They could not restore her mind again.

Three Little Ones
and the Giants

Three Little Ones lived in a little house tucked away behind the walls of a giant's castle. The entrance to their house was through a long narrow passage. The giants could not reach them for they could not go through the narrow entrance. Here the Little Ones lived in comfort. They lined their house with fur and made their beds of feather and bits of paper. When they were hungry, they came out of their house through the narrow passage. They ran about the halls of the castle and took the food which the giants neglected. Sometimes the little giants dropped their cake or other food or threw it away. This the Little Ones were very glad to get and carried to their home behind the wall. They grew fat and sleek. They were happy. Often they played and scampered about the Giant's halls. They became very bold and saucy. It happened some of the little giants saw them, while at play. They chased them, then the Little Ones ran for their lives. The feet of the giants were fearfully large. One huge foot would cover a dozen Little Ones. No wonder they rushed helter-skelter through the narrow passage leading to their home, where they were safe. The giants saw the little passage, but they could not reach the Little Ones.

The Little Ones were so frightened that they stayed at home a long time. They became very hungry. Then they came out to look for food. They saw a pretty little house with food in it. Being very hungry they did not stop to think but ran in and began to nibble the delicious food greedily. All at once there was a click and a snap and the door of the little house snapped shut. The Little Ones pushed against it but it was fast. They ran all about the little house but they could not get out. Their hearts beat fast. They did not know what to do. They walked all about and examined the little house carefully and found that it was really a prison. Iron bars were all over the windows and doors and they could not break them open. They could only wait to see what would happen.

By and by, the Little Ones heard a terrible noise. Several young giants came running up to the little prison. The sound of their feet on the hard ground was like thunder. The Little Ones almost fainted from fright. One of the giants stooped and picked up the prison. He held it upon one hand and looked through the bars at the little prisoners. His great eyes and enormous teeth, when he grinned, were frightful. The other giants crowded around and made a terrible din with their feet and voices. The little prison with its helpless inmates was carried about and exhibited to all the other giants, big and little. All this time the Little Ones were quaking with fear in a corner of their prison.

At last the little prisoners were carried out of the castle to a wide open space surrounded by high walls. Many of the giants crowded in this place. Then the door of the prison was opened just wide enough for one to go out at a time. Then one of the terrified prisoners sprang out among the feet of the terrible giants, hoping to escape, and ran hither and thither, pursued by the frightful monsters. There was no opening in the wall through which to escape and at last the monstrous foot of one of the giants was planted square upon his frail little body. Every bone in his body was broken and his life was crushed out. Again the prison door was opened and another Little One rushed out. His life was also crushed out as was the first one.

The third Little One was doomed to witness the terrible death of his beloved brothers, and knew his turn would come. The giants had no pity. They were powerful. The Little Ones were weak and helpless. When the Little Ones ran with terror and screamed with pain, the heartless giants laughed and danced. The giants again crowded around the prison entertaining the last Little One. "Turn him out, turn him out," they cried. Then the largest and most terrible ogre of all seized the Little One by the nape of the neck. He held him up as you would a feather. He smiled to see the grinning faces of his tribe upturned to his. Then with a toss he flung the Little One high above their heads. He fell in the midst of the terrible creatures. He sprang this way; he sprang that way in hopes of escaping the awful feet of his pursuers. But alas! his poor little heart failed him and his strength was spent. He rushed blindly into a corner and there was no escape. A dozen stamping feet struck the helpless body and crushed it into a shapeless mass. Thus ended the lives of three innocent Little Ones who unwisely built their house behind the walls of the giants' castle.

Yellow Hair and Blue Eyes

There was once a little boy whose name was Tommy Fane. He had a little sister who was only four months old. Tommy loved his sister very much, but he would have loved her more if she had had yellow hair and blue eyes. Her hair and eyes were black like Tommy's. Tommy did not like black hair and black eyes. He thought it would be very nice if he had a sister with yellow hair and blue eyes.

There was a new house across the street from where Tommy lived. One day a family moved into it. While the people were moving things upstairs Tommy walked into the house to look around. The first thing he saw was a cradle. In the cradle lay a lovely baby with yellow hair and blue eyes. When Tommy saw the baby he said, "Oh dear! I wish our baby looked like this." Then he wondered if his mother would not rather have this baby than her own. He stood admiring the baby awhile, then he lifted it from the cradle. It was so heavy he could hardly carry it. He held it tight and took it home and put it in his sister's cradle. Then he carried his little sister over to the other house.

In a little while the mother of the yellow-haired baby came to take it upstairs. When she looked into the cradle, she saw it was not her own baby lying there. She was very much frightened and thought somebody had stolen her baby. She took up the baby and ran across the street to tell somebody what had happened. She did not know Tommy's mother but she walked right into the house forgetting to knock at the door. There she saw Tommy showing his mother the new little sister with yellow hair. The strange lady was very glad to get back her baby and so was Tommy's mother. Both mothers cried a little at first, but they laughed when Tommy explained to them why he had changed the babies. They did not scold Tommy for they knew he had not meant to do wrong. They were sorry he had made so much trouble.

Dining-Room Talk

The dining-room was closed and the curtains drawn down. The chairs were in their accustomed places and the table presented its usual tidy appearance.

Everything was quiet and the clock on the mantel was humming its usual song, "Tick-tock, tick-tock."

All at once a deep sigh was heard from one corner and all looked in the direction and saw the head chair leaning forward as if in pain and a groan followed the sigh.

"Why, what in the world is the matter?" exclaimed the table, fluttering its white covering in an important manner.

"Matter enough," replied the chair. "I am sick and weary of this hard, monotonous life."

"That is what I say," piped one of the smaller chairs and all the rest echoed its words.

"Ah," sighed the head chair, "This life is almost unendurable."

"Well," inquired the table, "what special trials of life have you that others have not, I should like to know?"

"Trials! Yes, trials indeed!" exclaimed the chair. "Am not I and all my kindred constantly sat down upon? Are we not constantly held down and ground under burdens almost beyond our strength. Have not many of us actually broken down with the loads piled upon us. But it is not the burdens alone that we have to bear. We are pushed and kicked about in a manner to bring the blush of shame upon us. It is bad enough to be constantly supporting those creatures who go about on two legs, but when, as it often happens, one of them who weighs two or three hundred pounds, flops down upon us we are nearly crushed with the weight. Is it any wonder we groan audibly and shrink from such trials? If these creatures would only sit still when they are on us it would not be so bad, but when they wiggle about and push back and compel us to stand on two legs, or rock back and forth so we are kept jumping up and down, it fairly racks our frame. It almost breaks our back and makes all our joints crack."

Here a sigh passed among the chairs as they were thus reminded of the terrible strain they had all been subject to one time or another.

"What burdens can you have?" inquired the head chair still leaning forward. "You are treated with respect. You keep your place in the middle of the room. You are always kept nicely covered up and everything has to move around you and those two-legged creatures bow down to you as in worship. Yours seems to be an easy life indeed."

"Ah! Listen," replied the table, "and I will show you what I have to endure."

"In the first place my cover, which you seem to think so nice, is a burden, for it covers me up so I can hardly breathe. I am often seized by the head and foot and stretched out until I am on the point of breaking in two. Then the maid brings in the roast and places it square on my head and right beside it, she places a huge pile of plates.

"On my foot there is another pile of plates and other dishes, so with these weights I can move neither head nor foot. Besides this a row of plates and dishes are ranged along my sides and piled upon my back and some of them are so hot as to raise huge blisters on my delicate skin. Added to all these my little masters sit about me and jab me in the sides with their forks and spill hot tea and gravy upon me, and I cannot raise the cover to cool the burns. My legs are often kicked and the skin knocked off. Now are not all these worse burdens than you have to bear?"

"No, no," replied the head chair, "I have not told you all by any means. Sometimes we are thrown down by Sarah, the maid, with such violence that we bump our heads very hard on the floor. And only the other day when the nurse was out at the corner talking to Bobby, the policeman, master Tommy came in and pulled me down upon my knees, tied a leather thong around my ears for reins and then climbed upon my back and beat me with a cane. My ribs were almost broken and my back was terribly scratched. For this I was consoled, however, for when the nurse came in she shook Tommy real hard and took him away to the nursery."

"Tut, Tut," said the clock. "All this talk will not help you nor make your burdens lighter. Every one has his work to do and the best way is to be patient and keep pegging away, as I do."

Saying this, the clock struck six and the chairs and table became very quiet and looked very grave as the dining-room maid came in, let in the sunlight and prepared for tea. She never suspected that a mutiny had almost taken place.

Father Pumpkin

In Cairo there lived a worthy Mohammedan. He was industrious and frugal but extremely poor. He tried his best to support his family in plenty but he never succeeded. At last he began to complain saying, "However I may toil and plan, the wolf is ever howling at my door." He saw that thieves and rascals always prospered so he began to doubt the justice of Providence. He talked to his wife, Fatama, and grumbling said, "Mohammed is Allah's prophet, but what has Mohammed done to help boil my kettle, I would like to know. The thieves fare better and I am inclined to follow their business henceforth."

"Dog of an Arab!" cried his pious wife, "would you steal to better your means, and hasten Allah's vengeance?" She bade him arouse for shame and cease repining at his fate. She told him he must go to the Bazaar and take with him pen, paper and a book. She said he must sit in a corner, and look grave and solemn. He must read his book and make mystic scrawls upon his paper. He must pretend to be a wise man and learned sheik, then people could flock to him to purchase his advice. The man thought this might be a good plan. So his wife took a hollow pumpkin and placed it upon her husband's head. It made him look odd and grave. Then she bade him go off to the Bazaar and do as she had told him.

The man obeyed his wife and going to the Bazaar selected a quiet nook. There he sat and pored over his book with many a grimace and mystic look. Soon a customer appeared. It was a peasant in much distress. He said, "Good Father Pumpkin, I have lost my ass. You surely can tell me where to find him." Now the man was much puzzled. He knew nothing about the ass and he began to scold Fatama for sending him there. At last, in despair, he told the peasant to go to the graveyard for his ass. The peasant went there and found his ass. He was delighted. He returned and paid the sheik well. Father Pumpkin was surprised also, but he was glad. With his money he hastened home. He thought he had a wise wife.

Next morning Father Pumpkin hastened to his post. Many persons had heard of him and each of them had lost something and wanted him to help them find it. One had lost some money, another some silk, and another, a lover. With solemn face the sheik told each one where to find what was lost. All turned out according to his advice. Thus it continued for many days and Father Pumpkin became famous and rich. He was afraid, however, his luck might desert him, so he spoke to Fatama and said, "We are now rich and I shall quit my place in the Bazaar for we can now live without more work." Just then a messenger from the Sultan arrived. He told the sheik that the Sultan had been robbed of all his costly jewels. He had sent for the sheik to come to the capital and find the robbers. The messenger told Father Pumpkin if he could not find the robbers, he would lose his head. Now the man was very much frightened indeed. He cursed Fatama because she had gotten him into trouble but he could not help it and had to go along with the messenger to the Sultan. The Sultan gave the sheik seven days in which to find the robbers. Father Pumpkin was in sore distress. He was sure he would lose his head. He took seven white beans and decided to swallow one of them at the end of each day. So at sunset he took the first bean, swallowed it and said aloud, "There goes one." It happened that just then the leader of the band that stole the Sultan's jewels was passing by. He heard the sheik's remark and saw the uplifted hand. He was frightened and ran away as fast as he could fly. He told his companions that the cunning sheik had found him out. The next day the robbers sent another man who walked past the sheik. Just then Father Pumpkin swallowed another bean and said, "There goes a second." The robber fled, amazed. The next night the robbers sent another man. As he walked past the sheik, he saw his hand raised and heard him say, "There goes a third." Each night the robbers sent a different man and each time the sheik swallowed a bean and said, "There goes another." So the robbers felt sure Father Pumpkin knew them all. They were in great fear.

They took the jewels and went secretly to the sheik. They confessed their guilt. They gave him the jewels and asked him to forgive them. They promised that they would rob no more. Father Pumpkin was very glad to get the jewels. He made the robbers swear by the Koran that they would sin no more. Then he sent for the Sultan and gave him the jewels. The Sultan was delighted to get his jewels again and gave the sheik money and presents. He also promised to give Father Pumpkin whatever favor he might choose. The happy sheik at once requested that a decree be published forbidding any one ever questioning him again of any matter, either great or small. It was done and Father Pumpkin returned home and spent the remainder of his life in peace and plenty.

The Youth and the
Northwind

Once upon a time long ago, there was an honest old woman who lived with her son. Her husband was dead and she was old and lame. One day she sent her son to get some flour. The lad got the flour but he was careless and did not hurry home. He put down the flour and ran about to play. While he was loitering, the Northwind came along and stole the flour.

When the lad came back to the place where he had left the flour, he was very sorrowful. The flour was gone and it was all they had. He thought they must starve. He wondered what to do. At last he ran off swiftly to the Northwind's cave near the distant sea. He demanded the flour. He said they would starve if they did not have it. "I have it not," the Northwind growled. "But I will give you this tablecloth instead." It was a magic tablecloth. When it was spread the lad might order any dish and it would appear at once. The boy was much pleased and returned towards home. In the evening he stopped at an inn just half way home. He showed the people what his tablecloth could do. In the night the dishonest landlord stole the magic tablecloth and put another cloth in its place. The next day the boy continued his journey. He reached home in the evening. He told his mother about the wonderful tablecloth. She did not think the cloth would do any good and wanted the flour. The lad told her it was well that the Northwind stole the flour. Then he spread the cloth and called for meat and bread and other things. But it was only a common tablecloth, so nothing came about.

Then the youth was angry and hied himself back to the Northwind's cave. Said he, "Your tablecloth is of no account. I want my flour again." The Northwind declared, "I have not your flour but because you have no bread, I will give you this goat instead. You have only to say, 'Make money, master Billy,' and it will make all the money you want." Then the boy was glad. He took the goat and started home again. When he reached the inn, he showed what his wonderful goat could do. It made money for him. Then he went to bed but during the night the landlord stole the goat and put another goat in its place. The next day the lad continued his journey homeward. When he reached home he told his mother that he had a wonderful goat that could make money for them. His mother doubted it and said, "Your silly goat can do no good for hungry people." Then the lad exclaimed, "Make money, Mister Goat." But, alas! it was only a common goat and it could do nothing. Then the boy was very angry, because he thought he had been fooled again. He hastened back to the Northwind's cave and again demanded his flour. The Northwind was cross and said he did not have it. He gave the boy only a cudgel this time. He told him if he said to the stick, "My cudgel hit away," it would obey him and not stop till he told it to do so. The luckless lad took the cudgel and started home again.

He stopped at the same inn, where he had lodged before. He did not tell what his cudgel could do. He retired and pretended to sleep. By and by the thievish host came in and intended to steal the stick. The boy, who was not asleep, saw him and cried, "Stop, stop. My cudgel hit away." Then the cudgel hit the man on the head until he cried for mercy. Still the staff kept thumping the host about the head. At last he groaned, "I'll give you back your cloth and goat. Oh! spare my broken head." Then the boy told the cudgel to stop and he got his tablecloth and goat again. The next morning he proceeded homeward.

When he reached home he showed his tablecloth and goat to his mother. He showed her what they could do. After that they always had plenty to eat and lots of money. They became rich and the boy married a princess when he became a man. He had money for his friends and a cudgel for his enemies.

Alice

Alice was a little girl. She loved bread and butter and ate a good deal of it but she did not eat the crusts. She did not like them because they were hard.

One day a lady told Alice if she ate the crusts, it would make her hair curly. Then she ate all her crusts because she wanted curly hair very much. She thought curls were very pretty. She ate the crusts every day for a long time, but her hair did not curl. She was disappointed. She would not eat any more crusts. One day she ate several slices of bread but she left all the crusts. Her mamma reproved her and asked her why she did not eat the crusts. Alice said, "The lady told me, if I ate the crusts it would make my hair curly. I ate many crusts and my hair did not curl. The lady told me a story. I will not eat any more." And she did not.

Ginevra

Many years ago a wealthy man named Orsini lived in a beautiful villa near the city of Modena in Italy. Beautiful grounds surrounded his home and costly things filled the house. He had an only child, Ginevra, whose mother died when she was very young. Orsini loved his daughter very much. He watched over her carefully and never let her go away from him. She grew up beautiful, pure, and good.

When she was very young she became a bride. She married Francesco Doria. He was an only son and her playmate from childhood. There were many guests at the wedding. The bride was gay and happy and danced with many. She became tired and in a fit of playfulness, ran away to hide. She ran away from her young husband, laughing and looking back. She hastened to the attic-rooms of the mansion where many old things were kept. In one corner there stood an old, curiously carved, oaken chest. It was very large and strong. Ginevra ran up to this chest and opened it. She sprang inside and closed the lid. Alas, poor Ginevra! There was a spring-lock and as the lid closed, it snapped fast. The beautiful bride was imprisoned forever.

In the large dining hall the wedding guests sat down to the bountiful feast. Here was Orsini and Francesco; Ginevra alone was missing. All expected she would soon return. They waited, then they began to look about anxiously. Still Ginevra did not come. Fear and anxiety filled every heart. Orsini and Francesco searched everywhere for their loved one, but they never saw her again. The guests returned to their homes, sorrowful and sad. Francesco could not live without his bride. He went to the wars and flung his life away in battle. Orsini lived alone. His hair and beard grew long and white. Everyday he wandered sadly about his beautiful grounds and through the broad halls of his home. He seemed to be looking for someone. At last he died and his villa passed to strangers.

Many years had passed until one day some people who lived in Orsini's villa were in the upper rooms. Here they found many curious things stored away. At last they came to the large carved chest in a dark corner. They wondered what was in it. They moved it out to the light. It was old and worm-eaten. It was easily opened and the people were startled to find a skeleton within it.

Among the bones they found a string of pearls, a wedding ring, and a gold brooch with the name "Ginevra" engraved on it. Then they remembered the story of Ginevra and knew what had become of her.

A Cuban Amazon

An amazon is a female soldier. Long ago there were whole armies of amazons. They made good soldiers and fought and conquered like men.

It is said, in Cuba many women fight with the Cubans against the Spaniards, and some are braver and fight better than the men. These Cuban amazons are colored women. Their limbs are strong and their tongues are sharp. They can use the machete, revolver, rifle or knife as well as the men. Their dress is very simple. Usually it is only one cotton garment without shoes or stockings.

Not long ago in a battle with the Spaniards a woman appeared in the front ranks of the Cubans and fought bravely. She fired her rifle as often and as accurately as the men. She was a tall, fine looking woman. By and by the Cubans began to retreat. They ran away and scattered among the trees and vines. The amazon did not run. She held her ground. She called on the fleeing Cubans to stay and fight like men, but they did not heed her. Then she taunted them and called them cowards. The Spaniards came closer and closer. The woman was alone. She stood with her back against a tree and determined to die, fighting for her country. She shouted, "Long live free Cuba!" She loaded and fired her rifle at the Spaniards as fast as she could, and kept them back. After awhile her gun got out of order. She threw it down and drew her revolver. The Spaniards ran up closer, firing at her as they came. When they were near enough the brave woman cheered again and opened fire with her revolver. She kept on firing until she fell, pierced by several bullets. The enemy rushed upon her. As they did so, the wounded amazon raised herself upon her elbow and fired her last shot at the nearest soldier, killing him instantly. She then sank upon the ground and expired with a faint cheer upon her lips.

This woman was a real heroine and a patriot. She showed that a woman may die bravely for her country as well as a man. She gave the Cubans an example of courage that they might well imitate.

Four Brothers

There were four brothers. Said the eldest, "I want to be useful and do some good in the world. I will make bricks for they are useful things, so I will be doing something."

The second brother would not make bricks. It was too humble. A machine would make them. He would be a bricklayer and become a master bricklayer in time. He thought that was something better than making bricks.

"The master bricklayer is nothing much," said the third brother. "You will only be counted among common men. I will be an architect and people will think I am smart. *That is something.*"

The fourth brother turned up his nose at the humble occupations of his elder brothers. He would not be so low. They were only drudges. He would be something grander. He would stand back and watch the others work. He would point out their defects and lack of sense. He would be a *critic.* Said he, "In every work there is something that is not right. I will find that out and find fault with it. That will be doing something real."

Time passed. The brothers pursued, each, his chosen course. The fourth brother kept his word and found fault with every one. He did no useful work himself but he was always busy with the work of others. Nothing was done right. He was eloquent. People said of him, "He has a great head but he does nothing."

The eldest brother was humble but very busy. He made enough bricks to build rows and rows of houses. He fed and clothed his family and had something left for the poor. There were many broken bricks and these were useful too, for he gave them to a poor widow who lived on the bank above the sea. Of them she built her hut and was happy.

The bricklayer employed many artisans and built one house after another until he had built a whole street. This brother lived in a fine house and the working people flattered him. When he died he was forgotten.

The third brother, the architect, lived in the finest house on the street which his brother had built. The street was named after him. When he died he left his name but only in paint on the corners of the street.

The critic outlived them all and he had the last word to say. At last he, too, died and his soul ascended to the gates of Paradise. There he met the soul of the poor widow who had lived by the sea. Said the critic, "What have you done and why are you here?"

Just then the gates of heaven opened and the angel led the poor woman in. To the critic he said, "What dost thou bring? In all thy life thou hast not made as much as a single brick. I can do nothing for thee."

Then the old dame spoke for him, "For the sake of his brother who gave me the broken bricks, mayst he not be admitted?" Then the angel said, "For the sake of thy brother, whose honest labor seemed most humble to thee, thou mayest have hope of heaven. But thou shalt not be admitted until thou hast done *something*."

"I could have said that in finer words," thought the critic, but he did not find fault aloud. That to him was *something*.

Uncle Sam

Uncle Sam is a queer old chap. He is very popular and his picture is often seen in the newspapers. He usually wears a high, old-fashioned beaver hat, a blue, claw-hammer coat with stars on it and red and white striped pants which are too short for him and are held down by straps. He is very tall and slim and wears a long gray goatee. His feet are large and his arms and fingers are very long. Perhaps you have often seen his picture. Uncle Sam is a very rich man. He has large possessions of land, gold and silver mines, and many large buildings and ships. His wife was a Miss Columbia and he has a very large family of children.

Uncle Sam was born about the year 1607 in a strange country and among a strange, savage people. He was a weak, sickly child and his parents were very poor. It was feared he would not live long. At one time he almost perished from disease and neglect. At another time he nearly starved to death. By and by he grew stronger and by the time his infancy was past he was robust and hearty. He was a very bright boy and learned very fast. He was also very independent and was always ready to fight for his rights. He would not let others abuse him. Sometimes he got hurt in his quarrels with his neighbors but he did not seem to mind it very much. When he was a youth he grew very fast, so fast in fact, that his clothes became too small for him. That is why his pantaloons are so short.

When Uncle Sam was quite young he took an eagle for a pet and of which he was very fond. Eagles are long-lived birds and he has his eagle yet. He carries its picture about with him all the time. Its image is stamped in silver and gold. The eagle stamped in gold is worth ten dollars. Uncle Sam often presents the likeness of his eagle to his children and takes great delight in the pleasure it gives them.

Uncle Sam is a cousin of a funny little man, named John Bull. John Bull is short and fast and wears a red coat and top boots. He lives on one side of a large fish pond and Uncle Sam lives on the other side. A long time ago John Bull claimed all the nice farms on both sides of this pond, and Uncle Sam had to pay rent and taxes to him. The land was very wild where Uncle Sam lived. He had to clear the land and build houses. Then these farms became very valuable and John Bull made him pay high rent and more taxes. At last Uncle Sam refused to pay any more rent and taxes. This made John very angry and they had a fight about it. During this fight each of them was knocked down several times. Finally Uncle Sam gave his cousin such a blow between the eyes that he could not fight any longer and he agreed to let him have the farm which he had improved. After this Uncle Sam began to get rich. He bought more land so that, now, he has one of the biggest farms in the world.

John Bull has a pet lion and Uncle Sam used to tease it and make it cross. He would twist its tail, then the lion would roar and disturb John Bull. He did not like it and they often had cross words about it. In 1812 John Bull interfered with some of Uncle Sam's boys while they were fishing on the pond. He made them get into his boat and help him. This made Uncle Sam very angry and he challenged John Bull to another fight. It was a pretty hard fight and each of them got a bloody nose. When it was over John Bull promised to let the boys alone when they were in their boats on the pond. After this Uncle Sam lived in peace for many years.

Uncle Sam's next great trouble was with his own children. Some of those who lived on the sunny side of his farm did not like the way he managed his business. They thought they could do better and teach the old gentleman a thing or two. They began to do as they pleased and would not mind him. He determined to make them obey his orders, so he called on his children who lived on the shady side of the farm to help him punish the disobedient boys.

Well there was a big fight because there were so many of them on each side. Many of the boys were hurt very badly but at last the little rebels promised to mind Uncle Sam and be good children again. Since this trouble, Uncle Sam has been very prosperous. He is very proud of his possessions. A few years ago he collected all the wonderful things he could find on his farm and in his work shops and invited all the people in the world to come and see them. He felt pretty big when all those people came to see him. He put on his finest clothes and his pet eagle sat on his shoulder and screamed.

Personal Notes

Missive to Alice (1912)

Dear Alice:—

"The days are cold and dark and dreary, it rains and the wind is never weary," and I am poring o'er my papers and books, while the mud-washed lanes are running like brooks. But the rains must come and the winds must go, for everything's ordered for the best you know; and while I am safe 'neath my own roof-tree, I am glad that Dame Nature is fair and free. She sends warm breezes in the silent hours; she is generous with her gifts of flowers. So from open window I view the cloud of orchard blossoms, that fairly shroud the old back lot, which was bare and drear, and they fill the air with their fragrant cheer; so what have I got to complain of, dear?

The rain rivulets on the boughs of the trees are rushing the flowers to cheer the birds and the bees and quicken to life the seed in the soil, which gives us our guerdon for patient toil. The sun, it will ripen the fruit by and by and dispel with the mist the sad fruit-less sigh; so may we rejoice and smile at the gloom, while visions of gardens and fields in their bloom make us think of the time when you will return, and then shall I riot in things that I yearn.

And, dear, I am thinking of you in the day when the skies are blue or when they are gray. The rain does not dampen the love that is true and gloom's ashamed when I confront her with you. So, dear, do not fret when the lines fail to come just on time from the old Pennsy hill-side home; you know there are hearts that are yet full of love and dreams that are fragrant with thoughts from above, for the dear one away from the old roof-tree and all that are good they are wishing for thee.

Dad

My Connection with and My Activities at the Western Pennsylvania School for the Deaf

Note: We are happy to give our readers the following modest report on Mr. Teegarden's work in our school. The activities of this grand old man who gave almost fifty years to the school would fill an interesting volume.

The Editor, *The Western Pennsylvanian* [June 4, 1936]

In presenting this paper I did not intend to give a full history of the school but only my own connections, theories, and practice through my 48 years of service there, and my own doings as a shuttle weaving in and out through the various departments of the school.

The school as an organized Institution was founded by John G. Brown, D. D., who had taken great interest in the Pittsburgh dayschool.

As a residential school it was started at Turtle Creek in October, 1876, with Mr. James H. Logan, M. A. as acting principal.

I graduated from Gallaudet College, June 1876, and was appointed teacher on the recommendation of Dr. E. M. Gallaudet, then president of the college.

Aside from the principal I was the first teacher appointed to a position at the new institution. There I took charge of the highest class which then was composed of two or three divisions or grades about the middle of October of that year.

Besides teaching these grades six hours a day, I acted as boys' supervisor out of school hours. Also we had then two hours of study supervision in the evenings. So summing up I was on duty one way or another 8 or 10 hours daily for the first two or three years. Besides these duties I joined with the other teachers and the principal in writing and adapting popular stories for pupils' reading and these were published in the then popular *Raindrop*.

In later years I also wrote and had printed at the school another volume, entitled *Stories, Old and New*. These stories and others that followed were produced as a means to encourage the reading habit in our pupils.

At one of our teachers' meetings I presented a paper entitled "The Work Method" and argued that theories of instruction do not amount to much unless proved through earnest and energetic practice—that is, through earnest study and hard work. Much of this preparation could be done outside the school room hours. It did not strike my audience as of much consequence; it required too much concentration on their work and consumption of leisure time.

I spent one summer vacation in my Congressman's printery and learned the fundamentals of the printing trade and some time after that I was able to start the printery at the school. We began with a second-hand job press and a few trays of type. This was commenced in January of that year—1884—and by June of that year, also, we were able to print the Closing Day program as well as reading stories and news items. This service I volunteered without any extra compensation but the success of the demonstration induced the Board to pay me in part for the time spent and fixed a regular salary for the following years. I continued as instructor and started the school's regular publications.

The growth and work of the printery in addition to my regular classroom work was getting too big for me so I retired for one who could give his whole time to the business. This finally came to Mr. H. L. Branson, a thorough-going printer in all departments. He was also editor of school publications.

Later on when Mr. Branson's health failed, I was put in charge of the enlarged printery while he took a vacation. He did not last long, however, after he returned and I was again shoved into the printery.

The next comer was Mr. A. D. Hays but because of failing health he did not last long and retired in December of the same year. In January I was shoved into the office again and carried on till the close of school in June.

Other printers came and went and as before I was there to wait for their successors.

All my life I was interested in carpentry and cabinet-making so when the Board decided to start the industrial departments, I was able to introduce the first carpenter and cabinet maker in the person of Mr. A. A. Jack: also the wood carver, Mr. A. Seidel. Samples of their teaching and work are still about the apartments.

There were other interests about the school that I helped to advance but this is sufficient to show my whole-hearted interest in the school and its products.

George M. Teegarden

A Pleasant Summer Trip
(1916)

I have never been much of a traveller. Homeland has always seemed good enough for me, so when I was persuaded to try a 3,600-mile cruise on the Great Lakes I had some misgivings; but when it was all over I could but admit it was something worthwhile.

The trip was made under most auspicious circumstances. During the hottest spell the first part of August the twelve days on the lakes were most agreeable and pleasant from end to end. No rough weather was encountered and the lakes, they said, were unusually placid and smooth, although it was cool enough for overcoats at times.

We boarded the South American at Cleveland and sailed to Buffalo during the night. Having a whole day at the latter city, we trollied to Niagara Falls and viewed again these famed wonders of nature. From Buffalo we proceeded to Detroit, that city where automobiles are turned out by the thousands every day. In the Ford establishment one group of workmen assemble an auto every twenty minutes and there are many such groups working at the same time to turn out their enormous output.

The sail through Lake St. Clair, the St. Clair ship canal and past the noted St. Clair Flats was full of interest and novelty. The lines of summer cottages and hotels which border the channel and St. Clair Flats seemed, from the steamer, to be a foot or so above the water and are separated singly or in groups by passages or canals, so that boats are necessary for intercourse. It was all very interesting.

Across Lake Huron we reached Mackinaw Island where another picture is presented. Its village, magnificent hotel, and high, rocky bluffs, crowned with old block houses and barrack buildings are worth seeing. Here is one spot where the auto has not invaded nature's domain. They are excluded and the horse is still king. One half of the island is reserved for a state park and presents many features of scenic beauty.

The St. Mary's river, the cities of Soo, the rapids and the great Soo locks through which hundreds of steamers pass daily, were all full of interest.

Crossing Lake Superior we neared the northwestern coast on the way to Ft. William at the head of Canadian navigation. Land appears and we think we will soon be in port, but for hours the same headland seems as far off as ever. No wonder, for this was Thunder Cape towering up 1,400 feet, guarding the entrance to Thunder Bay, on the shores of which Fort William and Fort Arthur are developing into mighty cities. Just behind Thunder Cape is the Sleeping Giant, a curiously shaped island which from the bay resembles a mighty figure seemingly at rest.

Duluth was reached in the early morning when the sun revealed the city in all her glory. We cannot begin to tell of all that interested us here. From the boulevard drive along the crest of her mighty hill we got a view of much of the beauty and interests of the city.

A bird's eye view revealed East Duluth, her ore docks, lumber docks, grain elevators, line upon line of ore trains, ore steamers coming and going, and other features, all of which presented Duluth's commercial enterprise and greatness.

The 30,000 islands in Georgian Bay cannot be forgotten. Transferring to a smaller steamer we threaded our way in and out and around thousands of islands, large and small, some bare rock, others crowned with verdure, some low, some precipitous, but all most novel and interesting. This seems to be the mecca for summer sojourners for thousands of cottages and hotels appear as we proceed from Penetang at the south to Parry Sound at the north.

Part Two

POEMS

On the Lakes

The waves beat roughly 'gainst the rocks
　　Of Superior's northern shore,
But long they've stood the thundrous shocks
　　Of the storm's relentless roar;
And Thunder Cape looms up amain—
The Sleeping Giant's guardian fane.

The steamers bearing ores, which mined
　　On Minnesota's shore,
They leave a trail of smoke behind
　　A-carrying valued store
For mills to forge in Vulcan bars,
In shapes for Eros or for Mars.

The gulls sweep round our ship, the while—
　　Their pinions never tire—
Their actions oft bring forth a smile,
　　And their graces we admire.
They soar, they dive and then they float,
Collecting morsels from our boat.

A million gleams dance on the wave
　　At near the close of day,
While our good ship so stout and brave
　　Speeds forward on her way.
Across the bosom of the lake
The sun declines midst pine and brake.

The picture clouds in gold and blue
　　Spread outward south and north;

A streaming sheen like golden dew
      Brings exclamations forth;
The wavelets dancing in the glow
Sparkle and gleam—a brilliant show.

The full blown moon hangs far above
      The waves that roll beneath,
A harbinger of hope and love—
      Its gleams the wavelet's wreath—
And here upon the inland main
Smiles on the sailor's fond refrain.

Memories

I loved the fields and the meadows green,
The shimmer and glow of the brooks between
Where the lowing kine oft quenched their thurst,
And the ewes their playful lamkinds nursed.

The billowing fields and the purling brooks
Were unfolded to me—my only books—
And barefoot I trod o'er hill, through dell,
Alone but happy, content and well.

Then, through the woods I roamed for flowers;
To memory these, delicious hours.
The shadows I watched in the limpid streams
Portrayed the life I saw in my dreams.

The caw of the crows, the hoot of owl,
The bleat of lambs, the cackle of fowl,
And the song of birds I loved to hear—
Ah, sweet all these to my listening ear.

Sweet, too, the blossom-scent from the trees,
And sweet the hum of the lusty bees;
But sweeter far were voices of those
I loved to hear at the evening's close.

The trail of the song went through my soul
As clear as the ring through the silver bowl;
And then my father's oft whistled tune,
As sweet as bird-warbles are in June.

These voices and scenes come back to me
Thruogh memory sure and reverie;
They're sweet indeed and true, although
They're voices and scenes of long ago.

En Reverie

En reverie, alone, alone save a cigar and thought,
    And there, amidst the loneliness,
    The curling eddies brought
Her to his vision from afar—the sunshine of her smile—
And fancy brought her happy laugh to cheer his heart the while.
In visions clear he sees her oft in moods both brave and gay,
    And e'en that smile his heart to bless
    Throughout the pulsing day.
He sees her image in the haze in varying forms that please—
Her look, her smiles come back to him, as a refreshing breeze.
Thus while his thoughts wing far away and smoke is curling up
    From his cigar—forgotten bliss—
    To sip a sweeter cup—
He fancies that amidst the scenes of joy and gaiety
She yields one moment's thought to him of love and sympathy.

The Blue Jay

See saucy Jay upon his perch;
His glance is keen, his prey a-search;
A scarlet sinner, it is true,
Yet he is garbed in brilliant blue,
As tho a bluebell came to life
With wings and beak for mortal strife.
We note the beauty and forget
The naughty deeds that we regret.
A noisy chap at times he is,
Yet we admire his brilliancy.

His deeds may well be classed as such
As mark the sinner's cunning touch;
But when we note the saucy crest,
The twinkling azure of his breast,
We think of Iris passing by
In innocence from out the sky.
When foraging he claims his rights;
He acts according to his lights.
He lives by theft consistently—
If he's condemned, may we not be?

The Boy of Ten

A boy, J. Easy, now aged ten,
Has been through Baby Land and then
To Boyhood Town he traveled on
And laid up toy-stuff by the ton,
As small ones do, and made his mark
In A B C's, and with the lark,
He rose up early in the morn
And waked the sleepers with his horn
But now at ten, his visions soar—
He's not content, but wants much more,
He'd journey on to Young Man Town,
An "Aleck" be in cap and gown;
He'd swell his chest and strut and gad,
He'd know a sight more than his dad;
He'd beau the girls and get in debt—
Perchance his ma would sigh and fret.
But those are stations on the way
From Boyhood Town to Glory Bay,
Beyond which is the Land-of-Men,
The journey's end for the boy of ten.

Gallaudet College
(Fiftieth Anniversary)

Hail Gallaudet! Thy sons and daughters throng
Into thy halls with laughter and with song;
In grateful homage, true, they praises bring,
And to thee, Gallaudet, in gestures sing.

Thou hast lifted aloft the cup of life,
Bubbling with hope and the strength of strife;
And they who have quaffed, shall they e'er forget
Thy most precious gifts? Hail Gallaudet!

Out of the shadows of darkest night,
From the length and breadth of this land of might,
And some have essayed the summits of fame—
Have trooped to thy fountains, the silent bands.

Many are marching o'er duty's rough road,
Thankful for sinews from Wisdom's abode;
And some have essayed the summits of fame—
Looking not backward except to thy name.

Hail, thou Gallaudet, guide of our youth,
Lead e'er thy children on to light and truth;
Thy scroll of fifty years bears naught but praise—
Shall it not last, in truth, through endless days?

A crown, Oh, Gallaudet, rests on thy brow;
Pride, Honor, Glory, Love before thee bow.
Ne'er shall thy spirit die, nor we forget—
Hail Gallaudet, thou Friend! Hail Gallaudet!

As They Pass By

The years skip on, they will not stay
        For aged folk like we;
They shower all our heads with gray
        And laugh at you and me.

The years, the little elfin years,
        They're never aged to be—
So let them laugh and flount our fears,
        They're always young, you see.

Ah, let the years prance o'er our beds
        And dance their dance of glee,
Their merriment shall turn our heads
        From gloom to fancies free.

We in our age may laugh and shout
        With youth and new-born years,
So let them come—crowd us about
        And wipe away our tears.

Kitty-Cat, Puss

Back in a corner dim and dusty
There is a hole, dank and musty;
    And kitty, pussy, catty, kit,
    Why by that hole do you sit?
"Mousy, mousy, mouse hides in there,
When he comes out he is my fare."

Birdie, birdie on the fence rail,
Kitty-cat, pussy curls her tail.
    While birdie sings his cheerful song
    Pussy, pussy, creeping along,
All of a sudden springs up high,
But birdie's message is, "Bye bye."

Pussy-cat, pussy sleeps in the sun,
Doggie, doggie comes on the run.
    Pussy wakes up, shows teeth and claws,
    Doggie comes to a sudden pause;
Pussy spits out her defiance
Doggie pausing, begs alliance.

Pussy-cat, puss, why do you purr,
Coiled in my lap and never stir?
    "It's nice and comfy and feels good
    To be petted and understood,
And so I purr with all my might
When lassies stroke my coat aright."

Questionnaire

Why do the leaves turn upside down,
Just before the rain comes down?

Why do the creeping serpents molt?
Did you ever see a white colt?

Why does the dog turn round and round
Before his sleeping posture's found?

How does the cricket pipe his song?
Why are "granddaddy's" legs so long?

What wood will bear the greatest weight?
What metal weighs the battle's fate?

The rope the tethered horse untwists,
Why it the cow all kindly twists?

Why do the sun-dogs storms avow?
From which side does one milk a cow?

Viewing the spring-time cherry tree,
Blossoms or leaves do first we see?

What are the kitten's whiskers for?
Why does the mouse have tail galore?

Why does the horse eat grass one way,
Why does the cow the other, pray?

When cows and horses rise, my dears,
Which is the end that first uprears?

Why does the rabbit in a chase,
Prefer uphill to lead the race?

Thorugh the woods or through the rye,
The cowpath's always crooked—why?

What creature gives us silks to wear?
What is its food, procured with care?

What food sustains the humming bird,
And how collected, have you heard?

How does the grapevine take its hold?
How does the ivy cling so bold?

On which side of the tree-trunk grows
The moss—and why do you suppose?

Why is the ocean salt and why
Does not o'erflow nor yet run dry?

But why ask more? The stream is long—
Indeed 'twould be an endless song.

Hallowe'en

Over the hill by the country-side
I viewed a field of pumpkins wide.
They lay on the lap of mother earth
And some were small—some wide of girth
Yellow and orange with streaks of red
For thus to color they had been bred.
They glistened there in the set of sun,
Jack Frost proclaimed their race was run,
And from the path thru groves of oak
There came a troop of goblin-folk,
Queerly shaped in form and feature
Led by an old, sharp-visioned creature,
And by some magic—a quick plan
Each goblin shaped a pumpkin-man.
They marshalled then in rows and rows,
And garbed then in fantastic clothes;
Then mindful of the magic wand
Some pumpkin-men took up their stand
Hard by the thicket of corn shocks,
Or in the shadow of the rocks;
While others scurred here and thence
And hid in corners by the fence.
The goblin-chief leaned on his staff
So solemn that it made me laugh.
Which caused a panic mongst the hosts
Of goblins foul and dead men's ghosts.
They vanished quickly from my sight
Thanks to the witching hours of night.
Succeeding, to the field there came,
A troop of creatures without name—
Some tall and slim, some fat and round—

Then from the shadows came black cats
And o'er them flapped a troop of bats;
The pumpkins all in a mad race
Came rushing to the meeting place;
Then such a dance I ne'er had seen
Was executed on the green.
Then at a signal every sprite
Vanished to meet again next night.

Anna Niblock Rankin

She lived beside a winding road,
They learned, who passed, 'twas Love's abode;
And they who paused, bowed down with grief,
Found in her touch a sure relief.

Just a woman without a creed,
Only that kindness was our need—
Her heart a garden of fairest flowers,
Transplanting its treasures into ours.

Only a woman with a heart of gold
Filled to the brim with gems untold;
Like as a lily that blooms in spring,
Cheering all hearts until they sing.

In tenderness we breathe her name
For Love was near where'er she came;
Her gentle tones allayed our fears
With music one more feels than hears.

Busy Bees

The bees are busy all day long
    Culling honey;
Their hum is loud, their fight is strong
    When it's sunny.

They visit all the blooms about
    And gather sweets;
For this through field and wood they scout,
    Nor 'voiding streets.

They are too busy, far, to play
    When shines the sun;
From early morn till evening gray
    Their work is done.

They linger not in shady bowers,
    As drones love most;
They carry food and feed the flowers—
    A busy host.

From flower to cell they oft return
    Ere day is done;
With burdens sweet they homeward turn
    At set of sun.

And humans love the busy bees—
    The good they do—
They love their stores in hive and trees,
    Now, do not you?

The Workman

We find him in the wood and field
    A-hewing and a-tilling;
He coaxes Mother Earth to yield
    Our shelter and its filling;
We know he delveth in the mine—
    A grimy, crooked gnome—
For coals and shining gold; in fine
    He warms and gilds our homes.

Behold him at the forge and mill,
    Bent down unto his labor,
A Vulcan in his might and will—
    A master, a creator.
We see him in our shops and marts,
    O'ercast with dust and grime;
He brings unto our homes and hearts
    Essence of rose and thyme.

He braves the perils to rear our domes,
    Risks health and limb and life;
The making of our meanest homes
    May e'en bereave a wife
He shrinks not from the hardest toil—
    His strength he does not stint—
From shop and forge and the rich soil
    He garners sweet content.

So of his brawn, sinew and bone,
    Aided by cunning crafts,
Our hearths, our wealth, our all have grown,
    And monumental shafts.

He toileth on at God's behest—
    Sinews attuned to labor—
With heartbeats true in manly breast,
    And true unto his neighbor.

Now see him as he strides along,
    In leisure moments free,
And as he mingles with the throng,
    His mien of modesty.
His garb is plain, yet e'en the while
    That fashions around him press,
You see his lips curl with a smile—
    His thoughts? Why, you can guess!

Flowers of Spring

Pussy-willows now appear—
    Harbingers of Spring—
Driving from our hearts the fear,
    Rousing them to sing.

Columbine and violets
    Peep from 'neath the sod,
Smiling thanks lest one forgets
    The graciousness of God.

In among the brambles, there,
    Blossoms white and pink
Scenting all the balmy air—
    Praising God, I think.

Man, shall he be less thankful be
    Than the tiny flowers?
He must sense divinity
    In their waking hours.

Our Alice (1906)

Her image lies before me now,
The essence of a grace that's rare,
The form, the brow, I scarce know how,
Portrays a life that's true and fair.

The lips that speak, the eyes that smile,
Say life is sweet and pure and good;
And so my heart they do beguile
And make me love her as I should.

I've loved her with a love that's pure
I've striven to guard her from all harm
My constancy, true, will endure
Through life's vicissitudes or charm.

The college cap and gown she bears
Set off the form and shines the face;
In this the heart most eager shares
To lend a charm and add a grace.

Can scarce believe our Alice grown
In ways that are so fair and free,
So few short years have come and flown
Since she was dandled on my knee.

She quits her Alma Mater now—
Out in the world with pulsing song—
The force she has we must allow
Suffice to keep her with the throng.

So brings she others cheer and hope—
A lifter brave of burdens here—
The spirit strong with wider scope
Than leaners have who doubt and fear.

So give her love—a woman's meed [sic]—
Give her your faith and loving trust,
For she'll be true—a friend indeed—
Till heart and brain dow down to dust.

Rhymes for a Party

What, make a rhyme,
That true will chime
In with your joys at festal time!
The muses call up one by one,
The gnomes, the fays, all canny broods,
And tickle each to get some fun,
Though unfamiliar with their moods,
Their nectar quaff,
And make you laugh
With tales spun out on their distaff!

What can the fad
Of rhymsters add
To other charms and make you glad?
The great god Pan blew on his reeds
And charming tunes flew west and east,
Drowning the toots of lesser breeds,
Through he, in truth, were half a beast.
'Tis all the same,
He made a name.
And that's the surest way to fame.
So shall not I
Attempt or try
Add to the bliss provided by
A spinster Y., a mistress B.,
Who each can spout a done-brown toast,
Or a Mrs. S. and a matron D.,
Each in herself a goodly host.
They're great, allow,
To them I bow
So will you please excuse me now.

Gotham

I've trod through Gotham's busy streets—
    Burrowed beneath her rocks—
I've seen her wondrous shipping fleets
    And her maidens' gorgeous frocks;
I've stood upon her rock-ribbed hills
    And viewed her reaches wide;
I've had a taste of all her thrills—
    Some of her ills beside.

I marveled at her towering hives
    Where human swarms abide;
I traveled o'er her stately drives
    Where wealth and power reside;
I saw amazing sights by day
    Along the swelling tide;
By arches grand—an aerial way—
    Through space I seemed to glide.

And then when Folly claimed my view—
    Exampled at the shore—
My fancy ne'er had dared to woo
    Such wondrous things before!
"The great white way" made its impress—
    the midnight's glittering show—
I ne'er had dreamed such gorgeousness—
    A million stars aglow.

To the City Toiler

Away from the dust and the grime of the street,
    Away from the jangle and noise;
Away from the rush and clatter of feet,
    Away from the lure of "the boys."
Come out to the woods and wide meadows sweet,
    Come near to nature's employs;
Get down to the brooks where the waters are sweet
    With rod and reel for your toys.

Away from the mills and excitement of marts,
    Away from the factory's din;
Away from the smoke and the toil's weary smart,
    Away from the surgings within.
Come out to the streams where the kingfishers dart
    At sight of a flashing fin;
Get out to the "wild" and the copse's deep part—
    Behold the redbreast and wren.

Then smile while you may, be it dull, be it gay
    And blithely sing an old song;
Contentment will sink in your heart by the way
    As you go plodding along.
Then laugh at the tricks of the frolicsome jay
    And hark, to the sylvan throng,
For music and sunshine will fill out the day
    Until the shadows are long.

The Clovers

The clovers have no time to play,
They feed the cows and make the hay,
And trim the lawns and help the bees
Until the sun shines through the trees;
And then they lay aside their cares
And fold their hands and say their prayers,
And drop their tired little heads,
And go to sleep on clover beds.
Then when the day dawns clear and blue,
They wake and wash their hands in dew,
And as the sun climbs up the sky
They hold them up and let them dry,
And then to work the live-long day,
For clovers have no time to play.

Song Silence

No gloom there be by ingleside,
A silent song doth there abide;
The shadows dancing on the wall
Sing to us fancies great or small,
The stir of life within the clod
Creeps upward from beneath the sod,
And reaching out toward the sky
Its carol sings to cheer the eye.

The world's attuned to song for me
And all that grow sing sympathy.
There's music in the swaying trees—
The note is wafted by the breeze.
With smiling Nature we rejoice
In silence rather than with voice.
A silent motion charms the throng—
Where'er there's life there is a song.

The "NAD"

[After National Association of the Deaf]

The "Nad" is out of swaddling clothes—
He's lusty and his horn he blows,
      You bet.
We all will join this hustling band
Nor make our bow to voices "canned"—
      Not yet.

We like not the Procrustean bed,
Nor all with the same spoon be fed—
      We'll fight.
To check bad laws in this free land—
Stand by our cause so true and grand—
      Our right.

And east and west and north and south,
By every sign and word of mouth,
      We'll sing
The praises of the N. A. D.,
      And put to flight the enemy,
      A-ling.
If you're a Nad, why, that's all right,
You're numbered with the best tonight,
      My son.
      Are you a Nad? If not, why not?
Right here and now, upon the spot,
      Be one!

On Leaving "The Birches"

This morn we viewed a soothing nook
    Where quiet people dwell,
Amidst the groves of birch and pines—
    We grieved to say farewell.

A sparkling lake was at the door,
    A boat moored at the dock,
And oft we'd sailed from shore to shore
    'Round towering castle rock.

The mount above was steep and green—
    Huge boulders strewn about—
Where Titans played their game of bluff
    And put the Gnomes to rout.

The chipmunk and the groundhog dwelt
    Hard by the rocky ledge—
Their visits oft amused us much,
    Response to friendly pledge.

Groves of white limbed birches grew
    In front and at the rear;
The tree-toads and the katydids
    Added their mite of cheer.

The whole was a most pleasant scene
    And quiet were the hours,
Where books and music had their place—
    The joy was truly ours.

This peaceful scene of nature's charms
    Shifted to crowded streets,
As through by magic all was changed
    To cars and rushing feet.

A part now of the madding throng
    We rush from street to street,
Disturbed by whistles, clang of bells,
    And raucous sounds replete.

So back unto our burdens borne
    By duties stern and stark—
Withal a mighty rush of life
    Far from our lake-side park.

Spook-Night

The spooks will soon be on parade
With tricks and scares all newly made,
And to their aid as volunteers
They've marshalled kids of tender years,
Who in the dark would seek their bed
With trembling and qualms of dread,
But strange to say, will lend their aid
To spooks and goblins unafraid,
And march thru gloom of darkest night
And tug and stain with all their might
At shutters, gates and grinning "Jacks"
And hoot and groan thru window cracks.
They'd rattle corn against the doors—
Sneak in and scrape beneath the floors.
All this and more, with lantern gleam,
To scare the girls and make them scream,
To darksome nooks the maidens hie
With glass and candle held on high
To see the shadow of their love,
Lured by the spooks from groves above;
Or o'er their heads a peel they fling
And read their fate, the letters bring.
'Tis strange they brave the shades of hell,
All for the fancies spooks may tell.

Sir Robin's Inspection

A robin in my cherry tree
        Was flitting here and there
Inspecting all the swelling buds
        Apparently with care;
And up and down the boughs he peered
        With a gravity most rare,
Then cocked his head and seemed to say
        "Cherries there'll be to spare!"

A smile upon his countenance,
        My fancy soon detected;
His satisfaction seemed to prove
        The tree was well inspected.
He tossed his head in very glee
        The buds had been protected,
And seemed to taste the flavor of
        June cherries, ripe, expected.

He and his brothers claim that tree,
        Though we thought we owned it,
And long disputed we their claim
        With not a little credit.
At length a compromise we made
        That well required some wit—
Our share, a pie or two—no more—
        All else their benefit!

The Memory Window

The window of my memory wide open is today;
I see the old school on the hill, the boys and girls at play.
In their homespun and their ginghams they romp through dewy
    grass,
Nor heeding much the dampness—barefoot are lad and lass.

From this window I look out upon the hilltops and the streams
Where I roved in free abandon in those distant days of dreams;
And I see the shadows lengthen and the minnows in the pool
From the grapevine swing upon the bank—those days I strayed from
    school.

From out this memory window, I behold a maiden fair,
With braids of golden tresses—the sunlight lingering there.
And I see the color deepen on that brow of modesty,
And I wonder if she 'members all the trysts she braved for me.

'Neath yonder scrub I see a lad a-floundering through the snow,
In his coonskin cap and mitts and scarf breasting the winds that
    blow,
All for the rabbit and the grouse which dangle from his gun;
His cheeks are red and his eyes are bright, because he's had such fun.

And then I see the meadows wide and the reapers bent at work—
It matters not if the sun shines hot, no one is there a shirk.
I see the ricks of hay pile up and the rows of golden grain,
And the hurry and the scurry when the storm-clouds presage rain.

Ah, me, there are so many scenes, I see from this window fair,
So many things I'd long forgot in those ancient days back there.
Then I close the memory window and return to life, it seems,
For the past must flow forgotten with the onward rush of streams.

When I Am Dead

When I am dead, I hope to be
    Remembered—this is true—
Not for my wit or vanities
    But what I did for you.
I trust my friends will think of me
    And miss me some when gone,
Not for my virtues or my faith,
    Nor for my native brawn,
But for the efforts I have made
    To clearly spread the Truth
And bring the Light to darkened minds
    And hopeful strength to youth.

The flowers of love I oft receive
    While here I grope my way—
Then may you not upon my bier
    A single blossom lay.
A love for man is in my heart,
    And thankfulness most true
For all the blessings I receive—
    For love of God and you.
Then let me rest beneath the sod
    Within my narrow bed,
And fill your hearts with joyous thought
    Of me, when I am dead.

When I return this borrowed life
    No sorrow may you know
For any thought or act of mine,
    More cheerful may you grow
In memory of some kind deed,
    Or loving thought expressed,

To cheer the drooping soul of some,
    As though at God's behest.
"He did his duty as he knew,"
    May this be truly said—
Then grieve ye not, nor tears be shed
    For me, when I am dead.

Sources

http://www.smokycity.com/about.html#Pittsburgh

MacLeod, Anne Scott. *American Childhood: Essays on Children's Literature of the Nineteenth and Twentieth Centuries*. Athens, GA: University of Georgia Press, 1994.

Teegarden, George Moredock. *Common Words in Different Senses*. Edgewood Park, PA: The Institution for the Deaf, n.d.

———. *Stories: Old and New*. Edgewood Park, PA: The Institution for the Deaf, 1896.

———. *Vagrant Verses* New York: Fanwood Press, 1929.

Van Cleve, John Vickrey and Crouch, Barry A. *A Place of Their Own: Creating the Deaf Community in America*. Washington, DC: Gallaudet University Press, 1989.

The *Western Pennsylvanian*. Edgewood Park, PA: The Institution for the Deaf.

About the Editor

Photograph by Louis M. Miranda

Raymond Luczak was born and raised in Ironwood, a small mining town in Michigan's Upper Peninsula. Number seven in a family of nine children, he lost much of his hearing due to double pneumonia at the age of seven months. After high school graduation, Luczak went on to Gallaudet University, in Washington, DC, where he earned a B.A. in English, graduating *magna cum laude*. While at Gallaudet, he learned American Sign Language (ASL) and became involved with the deaf community.

Soon after graduating from Gallaudet, Luczak moved to New York City. In short order, his play *Snooty* won first place in the New York Deaf Theater's 1990 Samuel Edwards Deaf Playwrights Competition, which Tactile Mind Press published in 2004, and his essay "Notes of a Deaf Gay Writer" appeared as the cover story in *Christopher Street* magazine (November 1990). As a result of that piece, Alyson Books asked him to edit *Eyes of Desire: A Deaf Gay & Lesbian Reader*, which won two Lambda Literary Award nominations. Deaf Life Press brought out Luczak's first book of poems, *St. Michael's Fall* in 1995. Tactile Mind Press published two of his books in 2002: *Silence Is a Four-Letter Word: On Art & Deafness* and *This*

Way to the Acorns: Poems. His novel *Men with Their Hands* won a first-prize grant from the Arch and Bruce Brown Foundation for Full-Length Fiction 2003. The book eventually won first place in the Project: QueerLit 2006 Contest. Suspect Thoughts Press will publish the novel in October 2007.

As a playwright, Luczak has seen thirteen of his plays performed in many cities, from New York to Los Angeles to London. Some of his plays include *Whispers of a Savage Sort*, *Hippos & Giraffes*, and *Love in My Veins*.

As a filmmaker, he directed the renowned ASL storyteller Manny Hernandez in his hugely successful DVD, *Manny ASL: Stories in American Sign Language* (2002). Luczak's first full-length documentary, *Guy Wonder: Stories & Artwork*, came out in 2003. His next documentary, *Nathie: No Hand-Me-Downs*, appeared in 2005. His second collaboration with Manny Hernandez, *Manny: ASL for a Better Life*, is expected to come out in 2007.

In September 2005, Raymond Luczak relocated to Minneapolis, Minnesota, where he is editing the forthcoming anthology *Eyes of Desire 2: A Deaf GLBT Reader* and finishing up his feature film *Ghosted*. His web site is www.raymondluczak.com.